... WALKS
IN DENBIGHSHIRE
AND FLINTSHIRE

Bus and Rail Walks in Denbighshire and Flintshire

Dorothy Hamilton

ISBN: 0-86381-998-2

Cover illustration: Castell Dinas Brân

First published in 2005 by
Gwasg Carreg Gwalch, 12 Iard yr Orsaf, Llanrwst, Wales, LL26 0EH
✆ 01492 642031   📄 01492 641502
🖰 books@carreg-gwalch.co.uk   website: www.carreg-gwalch.co.uk

Contents

THE WALKS

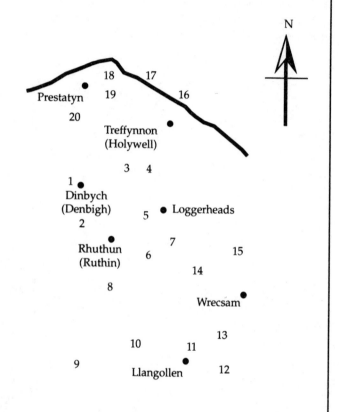

LOCATION MAP

N

Prestatyn

18   17
19   16

20

Treffynnon
(Holywell)

3   4

1
Dinbych
(Denbigh)
2   5   Loggerheads

7
Rhuthun
(Ruthin)   6   15

14

8

Wrecsam

13
10   11
9   12
Llangollen

Introduction

Denbighshire and Flintshire comprise an area of beautiful, varied landscape and historical interest which can only be appreciated fully by those exploring on foot. The counties are served by two railway lines and a network of bus routes. By making use of this public transport it is possible to take linear walks, which offer greater interest than circular routes.

The walks in this guide are suitable for those who already regularly use public transport, and for people who are willing to park their car for a while and catch a bus to the start of a walk, and walk back to their vehicle. Making greater use of public transport for trips to the countryside helps both the environment and the local economy, whilst arriving at one's destination on foot gives a certain satisfaction not obtained on circular walks.

Walks numbered 1-8 are in the Vale of Clwyd or cross the Clwydian range. The starts of these walks (with the exception of No.5, which uses a seasonal bus), are easily accessed by catching a bus from either Dinbych (Denbigh) or Rhuthun (Ruthin). Buses starting from Rhyl link the north Wales coast and its railway line with towns in the Vale of Clwyd. The vale can also be accessed by buses from Corwen, Llangollen, Yr Wyddgrug (Mold) and Wrecsam. Wrecsam is served by the Chester-Shrewsbury railway line and the Borderlands (Bidston-Wrecsam) line.

Walks 11 and 12 start or finish at stops on the Chester-Wrecsam-Shrewsbury line whilst walks 9, 10, 11 and 13 are on the Arriva 94 Wrecsam-Abermaw (Barmouth) bus route. All these walks, and walks 14 and 15, are easily accessed from Wrecsam. The starting points of walks 16-20 are on bus routes starting from Rhyl and Prestatyn, and both places are on the north Wales coast railway line, which links with the Borderlands Bidston-Wrecsam line at Shotton.

Before starting out on these walks, it is advisable to obtain the current bus and railway timetables. These are available from Denbighshire, Flintshire and Wrecsam county offices, bus and railway stations and Tourist Information Centres.

The walks range from 3½ miles (5.8 kilometres) to 11¾ miles (19.2 kilometres) in length. The estimated time given to complete each walk should be comfortable for most people, but fast walkers may find them overgenerous. Others may prefer to allow a little more time for birdwatching, photography, picnics etc. Most of the walks finish at towns or villages with refreshment places, but on the longer routes it is a good idea to carry some food and drink for snacks along the way. The routes are on OS Landranger 1:50,000 116, 117, 125 and 126 and OS Explorer 1: 25,000 255, 256, 264 and 265.

Background

The first evidence of people living in Wales comes from the Pontnewydd cave overlooking Afon Elwy on the west side of the Vale of Clwyd. Teeth and bone fragments of three Neanderthal people who lived about 200,000BC were found, along with stone hand axes and scrapers. At that time, Britain was still joined to the land mass of Europe. Neolithic people used caves near Tremeirchion and Trelawnyd. Burial mounds from the Bronze Age – about 2,000BC – are on the Eglwyseg plateau above Llangollen. A patterned gold cape of this period has been found next to human bones and amber beads at Yr Wyddgrug. Celtic tribes from Central Europe came to Britain about 600BC and built Iron Age forts on the summits of the Clwydian hills. The Deceangli inhabited this part of Wales and they were attacked in AD48 by the Romans, who later worked lead on Halkyn Mountain and at Meliden. The foundations of a small Roman bathhouse can be seen in Prestatyn.

After the Romans left Britain, Wales was divided into small kingdoms. Christianity flourished and Kentigern founded a religious community at Llanelwy (St Asaph). A large monastery was established on the English border at Bangor-is-y-coed

(Bangor on Dee) but it was destroyed by King Ethelfrith of Northumbria in the 7th century. This part of Wales was a battleground. On the road to the Horseshoe Pass near Llangollen is the Pillar of Eliseg, which records the victories against the Anglo-Saxons, as well as Eliseg's ancestry. In the 8th century, King Offa built his great earthwork boundary, and Wat's Dyke was constructed further east.

For short periods, Wales was united as one country. In the 11th century, Gruffudd ap Llywelyn held Gwynedd and Powys and won the rest of Wales. He defeated the English in many battles and had a stronghold on Twt Hill (Rhuddlan). Eventually, he was killed by his own men, who carried his severed head to Harold, the last Anglo-Saxon king. The Norman Earl Robert built a motte and bailey castle on Twt Hill from where he extended his territory to Deganwy.

Battles continued between Welsh rulers and the Normans, and Owain Gwynedd built a castle at Llandegla in 1149. He and other Welsh princes defeated Henry II's army at the Battle of Crogen, south of Corwen. Owain's grandson, Llywelyn ap Iorwerth, became the most powerful of the medieval Welsh princes. He built several castles. After his death, his grandson Llywelyn ap Gruffudd eventually became ruler and Henry III recognised his title, Prince of Wales. Negotiations with the next English king, Edward I, were less successful and, at the Treaty of Rhuddlan on 10 December, 1277, Llywelyn lost most of his lands. Disagreements continued, and five years later Llywelyn's brother Dafydd attacked Penarlâg (Hawarden), and other castles. Llywelyn went south during the rebellion, but he was killed near Builth Wells. Dafydd fought on, but was eventually caught and brutally murdered in public – hung, drawn and quartered on the streets of Shrewsbury in 1283.

Edward I consolidated his victory by building new castles, and English colonists lived in the fortified towns. Rhuthun castle was the first to be attacked in 1400 during Owain Glyndwr's rebellion. His army attacked other castles at

11

Dinbych, Rhuddlan, Y Fflint and Penarlâg. The war was to last ten years. Peace came to the area in 1485, when Henry Tudor became king, and the vale prospered. More action took place during the Civil War.

Nowadays, away from the coastal towns, Denbighshire is a quiet, unspoilt farming county dotted with historic towns and small villages. Flintshire has a narrow industrial belt. Both counties offer much historical interest as well as superb walking ranging from riverside paths to high moorland with stunning views.

Welsh Place-names

The following words are sometimes used in place-names in Denbighshire and Flintshire.

Afon – river
Bach/Fach – small
Bedd – grave
Brân – crow
Bryn – hill
Bwlch – pass
Bychan – little
Cadair – chair
Cae – field
Caer/Gaer – fort
Canol – middle, centre
Capel – chapel
Carreg – stone
Castell – castle
Cefn – ridge
Celyn – holly
Clwyd – gate
Coch – red
Coed – wood, trees
Craig – rock
Croes – cross
Cwm – valley
Dôl/Ddôl – meadow
Drws – door
Du/Ddu – black
Dŵr – water
Dyffryn – valley/dale
Eglwys – church
Esgob – bishop
Ffordd – road

Ffridd – mountain pasture
Ffynnon – spring, well
Gallt/Allt – hillside, slope
Garth – hill, enclosure
Glan – riverbank
Glas – blue
Glyn – glen, valley
Golau – light
Gorsaf – station
Gwaun/Waun – moor
Gwern – swamp, alder trees
Gwyn – white
Hafod/Hafoty – summer dwelling
Hen – old
Hendre – winter dwelling
Heol – road
Isaf – lower
Lôn – lane
Llan – church
Llety - lodging
Llwybr – path
Llwyn – grove
Llyn – lake
Llys – court, palace
Maen – stone
Maes – field
Mawr/Fawr – big
Melin/Felin – mill
Moel/Foel – mountain
Môr – sea
Morfa – marsh
Mynydd/Fynydd – mountain
Nant – stream
Neuadd – hall
Newydd – new

Ochr – side
Odyn – kiln
Ogof – cave
Pandy – fulling-mill
Pant – hollow, valley
Parc – park, field
Pen – head, top
Pentre – village
Pistyll – spout, cataract
Plas – mansion
Pont – bridge
Pwll – pool
Rhaeadr – cataract, waterfall
Rhos – moorland, heath
Sarn – causeway, road
Tan – under
Tre/Tref – town
Tŷ – house
Tyddyn – smallholding, small farm
Uchaf – upper
Ysgol – school

Useful Phone Numbers

Traveline Cymru	08706 082608
National Train Enquiry Line	08457 484950
Denbighshire County Council	01824 706968
Flintshire Bus Line	01352 704035
Wrexham Bus Line	01978 266166
Loggerheads Country Park	01352 810614
Llangollen Tourist Information Centre	01978 860828
Prestatyn Tourist Information Centre	01745 889092
Rhyl Tourist Information Centre	01745 355068
Rhuthun (Ruthin) Tourist Information Centre	01824 703992
Yr Wyddgrug (Mold) Tourist Information Centre	01352 759331

Country Code

1. Guard against any risk of fire.
2. Keep to the public rights of way when crossing farmland.
3. Avoid causing any damage to walls, fences and hedges.
4. Leave farm gates as you find them.
5. Keep dogs under control and on leads in the presence of livestock.
6. Leave farm machinery, farm animals and crops alone.
7. Take care not to pollute water.
8. Carry all your litter home with you.
9. Protect all wildlife, plants and trees.
10. Avoid making any unnecessary noise.
11. Drive carefully on country roads.
12. Enjoy and respect the countryside.

WALK 1

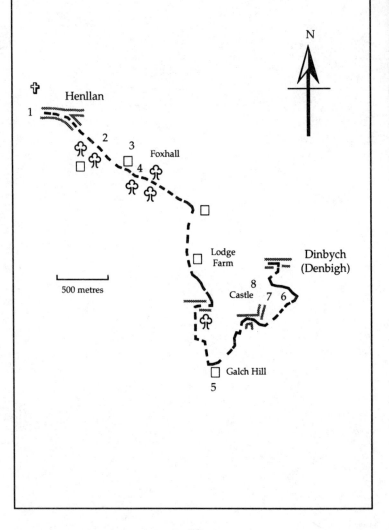

Henllan

1

2

3 Foxhall

4

Lodge Farm

Dinbych (Denbigh)

8 Castle

7 6

500 metres

5 Galch Hill

N

Henllan – *Foxhall – Galch Hill – Dinbych (Denbigh)*

Route:	Easy. Field and woodland paths.
Time:	2½-3 hours.
Start:	Henllan. Bus stops near the post office. GR 024681.
Finish:	Dinbych (Denbigh). Bus stop at Lenton Pool. GR 050661.
Public Transport:	Bus no. 66 Dinbych-Henllan-Llannefydd to the start. Bus no. 51 from Rhyl (trains) to Dinbych and from Rhuthun (Ruthin). Bus nos. 14, 14A from Yr Wyddgrug (Mold).
Parking:	Car park near Lenten Pool in Dinbych.
Facilities:	Pub in Henllan. Full facilities in Dinbych.
OS Maps:	1:50 000 Landranger 116; 1:25 000 Explorer 264.

Points of Interest:

1. The church of St Sadwrn in Henllan is unusual for its detached tower, which is sited above the church. One reason for this may be that the bells could be heard over a larger area than from the church below. The parish of Henllan was once sixteen miles long. The church was rebuilt during Georgian and Victorian times but it has a medieval east window. The shaft of a medieval preaching cross stands in the churchyard. Below the church is the *Llindir Inn* which dates from 1229. It is said to be haunted by the murdered, unfaithful wife of a former landlord.

2. Foxhall Newydd was a three storeyed building built about three hundred years ago by John Panton, a Recorder of Denbigh. He wanted it to be the largest house in the district, but he became bankrupt and it was never finished.

3. Foxhall dates from medieval times, but it has been altered and extended several times. Humphrey Llwyd (1527-1568) was born at Foxhall and he became the private physician to the Earl of Arundel. On his return to Dinbych, he lived at the castle. He was a cartographer and his maps were included in an atlas published by the Dutch geographer Ortelius in 1573.

4. The Iron Age enclosure is visible as a bank less than a metre high and about sixty metres in diameter. There are also two parallel banks to the south-west. It was probably a farmstead.

5. Sir Thomas Myddleton (1550-1631) and Sir Hugh Myddleton (1560-1631) were born at Galch Hill. Their father was Richard Myddleton, governor of Denbigh castle. Both were merchant adventurers and MPs. Sir Thomas became Lord Mayor of London in 1613. Sir Hugh was an engineer, and he built the 38 mile waterway which takes water from springs near Ware, Hertfordshire to London.

6. The lordship of Denbigh was given in 1563 to Robert Dudley, Earl of Leicester. He intended to build a large, Protestant church within the town walls. The foundation stone was laid in 1578, but building was slow due to lack of money and support, and the church was never finished.

7. Built about 1300, St Hilary's church was a large building with a crypt. It was rebuilt in the early 18th century, and only fell into disuse in 1874 when a new church was built for the town. It was finally demolished in 1923 and only the tower remains.

8. A castle built by Dafydd ap Gruffudd previously stood on the site of the present Denbigh castle. After Edward I's final conquest of Wales, Henry de Lacy, the Earl of Lancaster, was granted the lordship of the area and he built the present castle and town walls. Whilst under construction, the castle was taken for a short period by the Welsh during a revolt led by Madog

ap Llywelyn. However, it held out against Owain Glyndŵr's rising. During the Wars of the Roses the town was burnt within the walls and, perhaps because of the disaster, the townsfolk gradually moved from the hilltop and established a town on lower ground. Near the castle is a cottage that was the birthplace of John Rowlands, who later changed his name to Henry Morton Stanley. As a child he was in St Asaph workhouse but, after running away to sea, he changed his name to that of a man who adopted him. He became a journalist for the *New York Herald* and was sent to Africa to look for David Livingstone. He uttered the famous words when he found him: '*Dr Livingstone, I presume?*' He later returned to Britain, became an MP and was knighted.

Walk Directions: (–) denotes Point of Interest

1. After exploring Henllan (1) return to the bus stop near the post office and continue along the road in the direction of Dinbych for about 100 metres. Turn right at a footpath signpost and follow a lane uphill for 200 metres. At the end of a garden wall on the left, cross a stile into a field.

2. Walk along the left boundary behind houses to another stile, then take an enclosed path to a field. Continue along the right-hand boundary of this large field to a stile at a gate. Just before reaching it, look right to spot the ruins of Foxhall Newydd (2). In a few metres, leave the right-hand wall, and pass some trees on your left. Walk towards Foxhall (3) and cross a stile to the right of a wall.

3. Continue ahead through the field passing an Iron Age enclosure (4) on your left. Veer slightly right to a wall corner. Pass it on your right and go through a gate. Walk on through woodlands to another gate. Follow a clear path along the edge of the woods to a stile.

4. Walk up the field, slightly right, to a stile, then head

diagonally through the field to the far corner and a stone stile. Emerge on a road and immediately turn right along a lane. After about 150 metres cross a stile on the left.

5. Follow an enclosed path downhill then uphill to a stile. Walk along the left side of a field for a few metres and take another stretch of enclosed track. Follow it to a stile near Lodge Farm.

6. Walk ahead and pass farm buildings on the left. Walk uphill along the left boundary of a field to a stile. Turn right along the farm lane and emerge on the A543.

7. Turn right and in about 100 metres, at a layby, cross a stile on the left near a gate. Walk through the field following the right-hand hedge to a stile. Continue along an enclosed path to a stile and onwards to another stile and field.

8. Now follow the right boundary of the field, which curves to the left, to a stile. Pass a building and the house called Galch Hill (5) on your right then turn left on an access lane. In a few metres, cross a stone stile on your left.

9. Cross the field diagonally right and go through a gap to continue beside a right-hand hedge to a stile. Follow an enclosed path to a road. Turn left to another road, then bear right to a junction.

10. Bear right and, almost immediately, turn left on a track. In a few metres, when the track bends left, continue ahead on a path. Walk downhill and ignore a kissing gate on the right. Further on, have a railing on the right, and pass Goblin Tower on your left.

11. The path becomes surfaced and reaches a fork. Bear left uphill to another path then go left again. Emerge on a lane at a bend and bear left, uphill. Pass the remains of Leicester's church (6) on your left and continue uphill to the tower of St

Hilary's church (7) where you can go left to Denbigh castle ruins (8).

12. Return to the tower and walk ahead downhill to the Burgess Gate. Go through the gate to a lane junction and turn right along a dead end lane. At its end bear left down an alleyway and emerge in Dinbych town centre. Cross the road at the traffic lights and turn left to the bus stops at Pwll-y-grawys (Lenton Pool).

WALK 2

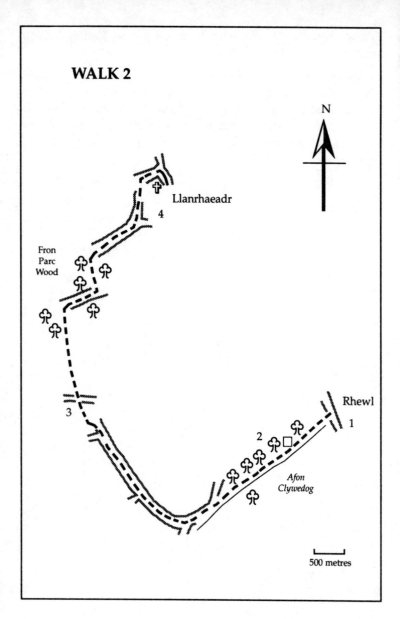

Llanrhaeadr

Fron
Parc
Wood

Rhewl

Afon
Clywedog

N

500 metres

Rhewl – Afon Clywedog –
Fron Parc Wood – Llanrhaeadr

Route:	Moderate. Riverside and woodland paths, quiet lanes and high pasture.
Time:	4-4½ hours.
Start:	Bus stop at Rhewl, near the *Drover's Arms* on the A525. GR 109604.
Finish:	Bus stop in Llanrhaeadr, near the church GR 081634.
Public Transport:	Bus nos. 51, 151 and 152 link Dinbych (Denbigh) and Rhuthun (Ruthin). Connections to Corwen, Llangollen, Wrecsam and Rhyl.
Parking:	On-street parking in Rhewl and at the southern end of Llanrhaeadr.
Facilities:	Pubs in Rhewl and Llanrhaeadr.
OS Maps:	1:50 000 Landranger 116; 1:25 000 Explorer 264.

Points of Interest:

1. The *Drover's Arms* was once a stopping place for drovers on their long journeys to market. Nearby is Capel Rhewl and the minister's house where once lived Emrys ap Iwan (Robert Ambrose Jones), a famous minister, writer and bard. Born in Abergele in 1848, he trained for the ministry at the Calvanistic Methodist Theological College in Bala. He spent the last six years of his life in Rhewl before his death in 1906. According to tradition, during the Civil War, Royalists and Parliamentarians fought a battle near the bridge over Afon Clywedog on the north side of the village.

2. The path beside Afon Clywedog is known as Lady Bagot's Drive from the time when it was a coach road and Lady Bagot drove along it in her carriage to Bontuchel. The Bagot family owned the Park Pool estate. There were plans in the late 19th century for the drive to be part of a proposed narrow gauge railway from Rhewl to Cerrigydrudion, but the line was never completed. Look out for the old limekilns above the path. Grey wagtails and dippers may be spotted on stones in the river.

3. The Mynydd Hiraethog and Denbigh Moors Path is a long distance path that starts in Pentrefoelas and finishes in Llanrhaeadr. Approximately thirty-four miles (54km) in length, the route passes through moorland, upland pasture, forest and tranquil small villages well off the beaten track.

4. The medieval church of St Dyfnog is known for the magnificent Tree of Jesse window which was made in 1533. During the Civil War it was removed and buried in the woods in the chest that now stands below it. Other interesting features of the double-naved church are the hammerbeam roofs and the marble monument to Maurice Jones of Llanrhaeadr Hall. His wife was a member of the Bagot family. In the churchyard is the grave of Edward Wynne, a Royalist from Llanrhaeadr, who was killed at Dinbych by Parliamentarians during the Civil War. His own regiment brought his body part of the way to Llanrhaeadr but, because the church was out of the Royalists' territory, Parliamentarians then took over and escorted his remains to the churchyard. Another interesting grave is that of Ann Parry who died in 1787. Many years later, when the grave was opened up for the interment of her son, the gravedigger found her body had been perfectly preserved. It was said that even the flowers placed in her coffin were still fresh. From the far end of the churchyard, an arch gives access to woodlands and a path that goes alongside a stream to St Dyfnog's well. According to legend, the sixth century saint used to stand under the little waterfall as penance and this gave the well healing powers. In

the eighteenth century, the bath was paved with marble and changing rooms were built around it. Pilgrims travelled many miles to bathe in the holy water, which was reputed to cure skin complaints. The almshouses beside the churchyard were built in the early 18th century. The pottery was once the old smithy, and the nearby inn dates from the 16th century.

Walk Directions: (–) denotes Point of Interest

1. With your back to the *Drover's Arms* (1), bear right in the direction of Dinbych and, at a road on the right (signposted Llanynys), turn left on a lane. Pass a farm and a house and follow a track through woodland. Afon Clywedog is on your left (2). Stay on the main track and pass a house. Ignore paths leading off.

2. Emerge onto a lane and turn left. Ignore a lane on the left to Bontuchel and walk uphill. Pass a lane on the left and, in another kilometre, you will pass on your left, the two forks of another lane. A few metres after the second one, cross a stile on the left (it may be difficult to spot).

3. Follow the right boundary of the field downhill. At the bottom, turn right beside a left-hand hedge. Cross a stile and bear left to another stile, but do not cross. You are now on the Mynydd Hiraethog Path (3). Turn right along the left boundary of the field and climb a stile at the end of the field.

4. Walk ahead to a track and bear left along it. It curves right to a gate and stile. Cross the field to another stile and lane.

5. Turn right for a few metres, then cross a stile on the left. Keep ahead through the fields, over stiles, until you emerge onto a track. Cross the track and go through the right-hand of two gates. Follow the left boundary of the field to a corner and go through the right-hand gate. Bear left beside a hedge and go through the second gate on your left.

6. Turn right to a corner stile. Walk downhill through the middle of a large field to a stile near a gate above coniferous woods. Join a track and bear right downhill onto another track. Turn right and, in a few metres, bear left to a stile. Walk downhill through the trees to a gate and turn right along a lane.

7. Follow the lane for a kilometre to a wood on the left. Ignore tracks leading into it but, at the end of the trees, go through a small gate. Walk downhill on a path to a forest track. Bear right above a stream and, in a few metres, turn right.

8. Walk uphill and cross a stile. Follow an enclosed path and cross a gap between two fields to another path. Emerge onto a lane and turn right along it.

9. The lane eventually passes through a golf course. Turn left on another lane and, in about 350 metres, take a path on the right into trees.

10. Cross a stile into a field and follow the right-hand boundary to a barn on the right. Go through a gate and turn left along the Vicarage drive. On reaching a lane, turn right downhill to a road then bear right to Llanrhaeadr church (4) and the bus stops.

WALK 3

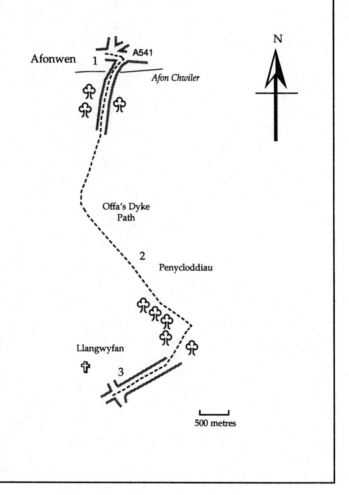

Afonwen

A541

Afon Chwiler

Offa's Dyke
Path

Penycloddiau

Llangwyfan

N

500 metres

Afonwen – Penycloddiau – Llangwyfan crossroads

Route:	Moderate-strenuous. Lanes, track, moorland and forest paths. Long gradual climb to the summit of Penycloddiau then downhill.
Time:	3-3½ hours.
Start:	On the A541, at the junction of the B5122 to Caerwys. GR 130715.
Finish:	Llangwyfan crossroads. GR 122658.
Public Transport:	Bus no. 14 Dinbych-Yr Wyddgrug (Denbigh-Mold) to the start. Bus no. 76 Dinbych-Llandyrnog-Rhuthun-Graigfechan from the finish. Buses to Rhyl from Dinbych.
Parking:	Lay-by on the A541 about a kilometre east of Afonwen. Car park in the forest above Llangwyfan. On street parking in Llandyrnog (1 mile from the finish). For this walk it is probably best to park in Dinbych and take a bus to the start and from the finish.
Facilities:	Restaurant at Afonwen. Pubs in Waen and Llandyrnog (1 mile from the finish but on the bus route).
OS Maps:	1:50 000 Landranger 116; 1:25 000 Explorer 265.

Points of Interest:

1. Situated in the valley of Afon Chwiler (River Wheeler), Afonwen developed as a small industrial village on the establishment of a wire mill and a paper mill that produced high quality paper for legal documents and banknotes. In the early 20th century, the mill became a leather works and, by the 1960s, it was producing textiles and woollens. Nowadays, the

building serves as a craft and antiques centre with a restaurant.

2. Penycloddiau is the largest Iron Age hill fort on the Clwydian range and covers about twenty hectares of bilberry and heather covered moorland. There is evidence of several huts inside the enclosure. The defences consist mainly of a single rampart but there are extra defences on the north and north-east sides. On a clear day, the hill offers extensive views. To the west, is the Vale of Clwyd and the peaks of distant Snowdonia. To the south, is Moel Arthur, with its smaller hillfort and, further distant, is Moel Fama. To the north, the hills stretch to the coast whilst to the north-east is the Wirral. From the hill, in spring and summer, you may hear, or see, meadow pipit, wheatear and stonechat.

3. If you have the time, it is worth venturing into the village of Llangwyfan to see the small, single chamber medieval church of St Cwyfan, with its simple interior and box pews. The churchyard contains the grave of Foulk Jones, who lived during three centuries, 1699-1801. Near the church gates are the village stocks. In the village there was once a TB hospital. During the early 20th century, a common cause of death in Wales was tuberculosis. Llangwyfan was thought to be the ideal location for a hospital specialising in the treatment of this chest condition, and the sanatorium with 226 beds opened in 1926. George V., accompanied by Queen Mary, performed the opening ceremony. As TB declined, other medical conditions were treated at the hospital until it closed in 1982. To the north of the village and church is the mansion of Fron Yw, which was the home of the Madocks family. William Alexander Madocks was born here in 1774, and he became MP for Boston in Lincolnshire. His interest in town planning led to the building of Tremadog in Gwynedd and the construction of the mile long embankment, known as Y Cob, across Afon Glaslyn estuary.

Walk Directions: (–) denotes Point of Interest

1. On the A541, face the B5122, and turn right. After a few metres, take a lane on your right. You will pass the entrance to the Afonwen Craft Centre (1) on your left.

2. Follow the lane uphill. After about a mile, when the surfaced lane bears right to a transmitting station, maintain your direction along a track. Further on, it becomes level and joins the Offa's Dyke Path, which is waymarked by white acorn symbols.

3. Go left over a stile and follow the path up Penycloddiau. Near a stile, there is a memorial stone to Arthur Roberts MBE, who helped the development of the Offa's Dyke Path.

4. Cross the ditches of Penycloddiau Iron Age hill fort (2) to reach the summit. Follow the path downhill through heather and bilberry plants to a stile.

5. The path descends along the edge of a forestry plantation to a small gate that gives entry to a car park. Do not go through but, with your back to it, go half-left and take a bridleway that descends between two tracks. It crosses a track and, further on, rejoins the track. Bear left along it to a gate and lane.

6. Turn right along the lane to the crossroads at Llangwyfan (3), from where you can catch the bus.

WALK 4

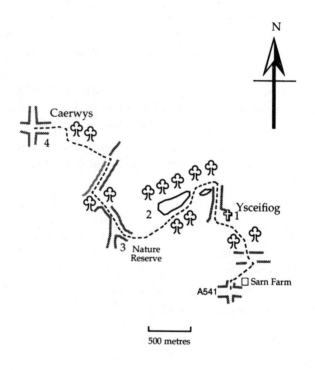

N

Caerwys
4

Ysceifiog
1

2

3 Nature
Reserve

Sarn Farm

A541

500 metres

Sarn – Ysceifiog – Ysceifiog Lake – Caerwys

Route:	Moderate. Field, woodland and lakeside paths, tracks and lanes. Gradual climbs to Ysceifiog and Caerwys.
Time:	2-2½ hours.
Start:	Sarn Farm on the A541 near the lane for Ysceifiog. GR 153706.
Finish:	Caerwys Square. GR 128729.
Public Transport:	Bus no. 14 Dinbych-Yr Wyddgrug (Denbigh-Mold) links the start and finish. Buses from Rhyl, Corwen and Llangollen to Dinbych. Buses from Chester (nos. 4 & 41) and Wrecsam (nos. 26 & 40) to Yr Wyddgrug.
Parking:	Caerwys Square.
Facilities:	Pubs in Ysceifiog and Caerwys. Public toilets in Caerwys.
OS Maps:	1:50 000 Landranger 116; 1:25 000 Explorer 265.

Points of Interest:

1. Ysceifiog church was rebuilt in the mid 19th century. This is an ancient site and the churchyard contains the remains of an old preaching cross. A memorial commemorates William Edwards (1790-1855), a local bard known as Gwilym Callestr, who won prizes at eisteddfodau. The first Methodist preacher in Flintshire was John Owen (1733-1776), who lived in the parish of Ysceifiog at a farmhouse called Y Berthen Gron, which became a centre of worship. Ysceifiog developed mainly as an agricultural community and is mentioned in the Domesday Book. Lead ore and limestone have been worked in the area. At

one time, there were three pubs, but nowadays there is only the 18th century *Fox Inn*.

2. Ysceifiog Lake was created to stock trout in 1904 by the Earl of Derby, when a dam was built across the Pant Gwyn stream. Nowadays, it provides a home for moorhen, coot, heron and swans. Golden-eye and other species of duck may be present in the winter.

3. The Ddôl Uchaf Nature Reserve is on the site of disused marl pits that used to supply clay. A circular path guides visitors round the woodland and wetland habitats. Plants that grow here include cowslip, wood avens, meadowsweet and grass of parnassus. In the summer, you may see several species of butterfly and dragonfly. A wide range of birds, including finches and warblers, visit the reserve.

4. Caerwys was once one of the most important towns in Flintshire, Edward I granted a charter in 1290, and the church dates from that time. Caerwys became home of the county assizes and had its own townhall and jail. Just off the Square is the Old Court, a Tudor house behind a later facade, where Flintshire Assizes were held until 1672 and Courts of Justice until the late 19th century. Another old building, on the corner of the Square, is Bell House where a bell was rung on fair and market days and for funeral processions. There is also a pinfold that was used for confining stray animals. Caerwys has a long association with eisteddfodau and two were held here in the 16th century, in 1523 and 1568. At that time, many vagabonds masqueraded as poets and minstrels.

Elizabeth I commissioned the eisteddfod that was held in 1568 as a means of distinguishing those with talent from vagrants pretending to be bards. A permit system was adopted that required performers to come to Caerwys and be judged by experts; those with no accomplishments had to return to 'honest labour'. The winner received a silver harp. John Lloyd who accompanied Thomas Pennant on his Tours of Wales was vicar of Caerwys.

Walk Directions: (–) denotes Point of Interest

1. On the A541, take the Ysceifiog road past Sarn Farm. After about 100 metres, turn right on a bridleway. Pass houses and walk uphill to a lane.

2. Turn left and, after about 100 metres, cross a stile on the right. Follow the field boundary to a wood and take a path through the trees to a field. With the wood on your left, slant uphill to a stile. Walk on through the fields, crossing stiles.

3. Cross a stile into the churchyard (1) and leave by the main gate. Walk down to the *Fox Inn* in Ysceifiog. Take the road signposted Babell and walk downhill.

4. After crossing a bridge, turn left on a path and follow a path beside the Pant Gwyn stream. On reaching a path junction, turn left and cross a footbridge and stile.

5. Bear right beside a fence and cross a stile into woodlands. Continue with Ysceifiog Lake (2) on your right. Eventually, the path climbs away from the lake to a stile. Bear right beside the fence and ignore another path on the left. Follow the fence to a lane.

6. Turn right and, at a fork in the lane, keep right. After crossing a bridge over a stream, you will see Ddôl Uchaf Nature Reserve (3) on your left.

7. Continue along the lane and walk uphill to a junction. Turn right and, after passing a house, take a path on the right into woodland. Walk uphill and veer left through scrub to a lane.

8. Turn right and, after about 650 metres, cross a stile on the left at a gate. Walk along the left side of the field for about 100 metres, then veer nearer the centre and pass a ruin on your left.

Cross a stile and, half-way through the field, climb another stile on your left.

9. Head half-right towards the right-hand lower corner of woodlands. Near the corner, take a path through gorse to a stile, then continue with the wood on your right to a stile. Take a path through the trees and cross a stile on the left.

10. Pass the buildings of Trout Farm fishery and walk ahead, uphill, to the Square in Caerwys (4).

WALK 5

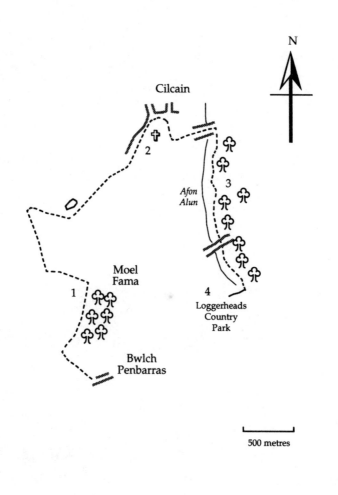

N

Cilcain

2

Afon
Alun

3

Moel
Fama

1

4

Loggerheads
Country
Park

Bwlch
Penbarras

500 metres

40

Bwlch Penbarras – Moel Fama – Cilcain – Afon Alun – Loggerheads Country Park

Route: Moderate-strenuous. Hillside tracks and paths, fields, woodland and riverside paths, lanes. Gradual climb to Moel Fama summit then most of the walk is downhill or fairly level.

Time: 5 hours.

Start: Moel Fama viewpoint. GR 161605.

Finish: Loggerheads Country Park. GR 197626.

Public Transport: Moel Fama Shuttle Bus from Loggerheads Country Park on summer Sundays from late May to late September. Clwydian Ranger buses from Rhyl, Prestatyn, Dinbych (Denbigh), Rhuthun (Ruthin) (Blue Line), Wrecsam, Yr Wyddgrug (Mold) (White Line), Chester and Shotton (Orange Line) serve Loggerheads Country Park during this period.

Parking: Viewpoint, Bwlch Penbarras and at Loggerheads Country Park.

Facilities: Cafe, public toilets and Visitor Centre at the finish. Pub nearby.

OS Maps: 1:50 000 Landranger 116;
1:25 000 Explorer 265.

Points of Interest:

1. At 1817 feet (554m), Moel Fama is the highest point in the Clwydian range, and offers extensive views in all directions. On a clear day, you can look west across the Vale of Clwyd to

Mynydd Hiraethog (Denbigh Moors) and the peaks of Eryri (Snowdonia). In the north are the Iron Age hill forts of Moel Arthur and Penycloddiau whilst to the east is the Cheshire Plain. In the south are moorlands and Llantysilio Mountain. The Jubilee Tower, on the summit, was built by public subscription in 1810 to commemorate the 50th year of King George III's reign. Several thousand people walked to the summit to attend the ceremony when the foundation stone was laid. Built in the Egyptian style by George Harrison of Chester, the original tower was 115 feet high, but after a series of storms it collapsed in 1862. Renovation work has since taken place, and there is a viewing platform with information boards to help identify distant landmarks. Look out for buzzard, kestrel and whinchat on your walk across the moor.

2. The church of St Mary is known for its splendid, intricately carved hammerbeam tussed roof. It is said that the roof may have been brought from Basingwerk Abbey. The churchyard is circular which indicates an early, possibly pre-Christian, site. *The White Horse Inn* in Cilcain dates from the 16th century.

3. Lead mining operations created the Devil's Gorge, which is a large chasm in the limestone cliffs. The lead mines were dependent on Afon Alun for their water supply, but as the river sinks into swallowholes in places during the summer months, it was unreliable. To overcome the problem, a three mile water channel was cut along the side of the valley from Loggerheads to Rhydymwyn. The mines were closed in the late 19th century, but the leat remains as a footpath. According to legend, the swallowholes were caused by a wicked ruler called King Benlli, who was punished for his sins by a burning sensation all over his body. He tried to cool himself in the river but, whenever he did so, the river disappeared. The woodlands are rich in wild flowers while dippers and grey wagtails may be seen near the river. Felix Mendelssohn stayed in the area and was inspired to compose *The Rivulet* whilst walking beside Afon Alun.

4. The area near Loggerheads has been known as a beauty spot for over two hundred years. The *Crosville* bus company bought a wood and two fields here in 1926 and brought in many visitors by bus after installing additional attractions. These included a bandstand, golf, croquet, swingboats, a boating lake, flower beds and a tea room. In 1974, the site was bought by the county council and it is now a country park. It is said that the name Loggerheads was derived from a dispute over mineral rights and county boundaries.

Walk Directions: (–) denotes Point of Interest

1. From the car park on Bwlch Penbarras, pass the viewpoint and go north on Offa's Dyke Path. Follow the obvious track to the summit of Moel Fama (1).

2. Leave Moel Fama by continuing, north-west at first, along the Offa's Dyke Path. Ignore other paths leading off. The path follows a boundary wall on the right over Moel Dywyll to a stile on the right.

3. Leave Offa's Dyke Path at this point, and cross the stile. Follow a track for about 100 metres, then go right downhill on a path. Veer left over a stream and continue on a path beside a fence and reservoir to a small gate.

4. Walk on along a track. Pass two small reservoirs and ignore paths leading off. Emerge onto a lane at a bend and go left uphill to the church in Cilcain (2). Turn right to crossroads.

5. Turn right and, in about 350 metres, go left on a bridleway. After about 100 metres, take a path on the left uphill to a stile. Bear right above a wooded valley. Cross several stiles and pass through some trees. Continue along the right boundary of fields, then take an enclosed path downhill to a lane.

6. Turn right and walk downhill. Ignore a bridleway on the right and cross the bridge over Afon Alun. Walk uphill and, in

about 200 metres, take a footpath on the right signposted Loggerheads. The path goes along steep wooded slopes above Afon Alun.

7. Pass limestone crags and a railed section. Further on, the path crosses a bridge over the breathtaking Devil's Gorge (3). Continue along the level leat path and pass the entrance to lead mines.

8. On reaching a lane, bear right to cross it and follow a drive. Take a path behind a house (kennels) and walk on through woodlands. Pass a sign for the Loggerheads Country Park and ignore a path on the left.

9. Continue on a path beside Afon Alun until you reach a stone bridge. Bear right across it to the Loggerheads Country Park Visitor Centre (4), cafe, car park and bus stops.

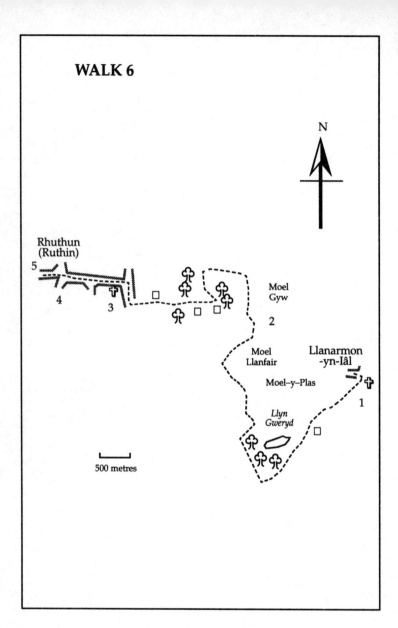

WALK 6

N

Rhuthun
(Ruthin)

5

4   3

Moel
Gyw

2

Moel
Llanfair

Moel-y-Plas

Llanarmon
-yn-Iâl

1

*Llyn
Gweryd*

500 metres

46

Llanarmon-yn-Iâl – Llyn Gweryd – Garreg Lwyd – Rhuthun (Ruthin)

Route:	Moderate. A gradual climb to the Offa's Dyke Path, which is followed north along the sides of Moel y Plas, Moel Llanfair and Moel Gyw.
Time:	4½-5 hours.
Start:	Bus stop in Llanarmon yn Iâl. GR 189561.
Finish:	St Peter's Square, Rhuthun. GR 122582.
Public Transport:	Llanarmon-yn-Iâl is on the B5 Rhuthun-Yr Wyddgrug (Ruthin-Mold) bus route. Buses from Rhyl and Llangollen to Rhuthun.
Parking:	On street parking near the bus stop in Llanarmon-yn-Iâl. Several car parks in Rhuthun.
Facilities:	Pub and shop in Llanarmon-yn-Iâl. Full facilities in Rhuthun.
OS Maps:	1:50 000 Landranger 116; 1:25 000 Explorer 256.

Points of Interest:

1. Dedicated to St Garmon, the church at Llanarmon-yn-Iâl stands in a large churchyard, which was once the site of a Celtic community. The building has some interesting features including timber roofs, a brass chandelier and some monuments. To read more about Llanarmon-yn-Iâl, see Walk 7, Point of Interest 1.

2. The Garreg Lwyd (grey stone) marks an ancient route between Llanarmon and Rhuthun (Ruthin). From this point a path – not a right of way, but obviously well used – goes to the top of Moel Gyw.

3. The church of St Meugan was the original mother church of the settlement which became Rhuthun. In the churchyard is the decorated shaft of a medieval preaching cross. Inside the 15th century church are several monuments to the Thelwall family of Bathafarn. The west gallery is dated 1721.

4. Well Street used to be called Welsh Street, as this was where the Welsh inhabitants of Rhuthun used to live. The English lived near the castle. There are several timber framed shops in this road dating from the 15th century. George Borrow, author of *Wild Wales*, ate roast duck in the *Wynnstay Arms* after walking from Llangollen.

5. Standing high on a ridge above Afon Clwyd, Rhuthun is a fascinating old town with a turbulent history. The name means *red fortress*. After decades of fighting, the Welsh settlement came under English control in 1282, when Edward I granted the lordship of Rhuthun to Reginald de Grey. In the year 1400, at the start of his rebellion, Owain Glyndŵr and his soldiers pillaged and burnt the town. The castle survived, and the houses were rebuilt. During the Civil War, the castle was held for Charles I, but was taken by Parliamentary forces in 1646, and subsequently dismantled. Near Barclays Bank is a famous boulder called Maen Huaill. According to legend, King Arthur and Huaill quarrelled and, after wounding Arthur in the leg, Huaill was beheaded on this stone. In the square is the National Westminster Bank, which was built as a court and gaol in 1401. The remains of a gibbet's beam is under the eaves. Near the Square is St Peter's Church, which was founded in 1310 by John de Grey. The double naved building has a fine 16th century carved oak roof and many memorials. Behind the church is a close, with buildings dating from the 14th century.

Walk Directions: (–) denotes Point of Interest

1. From the bus stop in Llanarmon-yn-Iâl (1) walk towards the

church but, before reaching it, bear right on a road signposted Llandegla. After a few metres, turn right on an enclosed footpath. Emerge on a road and keep ahead. At the end of the road, take a path between gardens.

2. Cross a stile and walk on to a stile on the left. Bear right beside a hedge and cross a stile in the field corner. Walk on to another stile, then head across the field towards the left side of a farm.

3. Climb a stile near a gate and cross the lane to a bridleway. Walk uphill and pass above pools and a house. Ignore a stile on the right and go slightly downhill. Cross a track and pass Llyn Gweryd on the right. Stay on the main track and, further on, have fields on the left. Go through a gate at the end of the track and, immediately, bear right to have views of the Vale of Clwyd on your left.

4. You are now on the Offa's Dyke Path. Climb a stile at a gate and follow the track uphill. Before reaching a mast, slant right to a stile. Part way down the hill, the path veers slightly left away from the fence and goes down then up to a stile. Continue uphill on a steep, grassy path. It veers slightly right to a fence and stile.

5. Follow a clear path through heather as it passes above a valley. It descends steeply to a stile and track. Turn left for a few metres, then cross a stile on the right. The path passes below Moel Llanfair. On reaching a stile and gate at sheepfolds, turn right uphill on a track.

6. Near the top of the pass, cross a stile on the left and take a narrow path to a wider path. The route goes left here, but you may like to go right for a few metres to see the Garreg Lwyd (Grey Stone) (2).

7. Continuing on the route, walk downhill to a corner and ignore a gate on the right. Cross a stile and slant slightly left

over two little hills, then descend to a stile. Head downhill to a stile in the right-hand corner of the field.

8. The route now leaves the Offa's Dyke Path. Go left through a gate onto a track. Pass Pen-yr-allt on the right and continue through fields to a stile and gate at a cattle grid. Continue on a track downhill through woods. Bear right near a ruin and farm buildings.

9. Have a field on the left, then enter the woods of Coed Plas-y-nant again, and walk on downhill. Ignore a track on the left to a house. Further on, pass a house on the left and continue along the access lane. Ignore a track on the right, then pass the waterworks and Bathafarn Farm.

10. On reaching a lane junction, turn right. Ignore a lane on the left and follow the B5429. In about 500 metres, turn left onto another lane. Cross a bridge over a stream and walk on to St Meugan's church (3).

11. Continue along the lane and, when it joins another, keep ahead. At a road junction go ahead and bear left to pass *The Feathers Inn* on your left. Either turn right along Station Road to the bus stops or continue along Well Street (4) to St Peter's Square in the centre of Rhuthun (5).

WALK 7

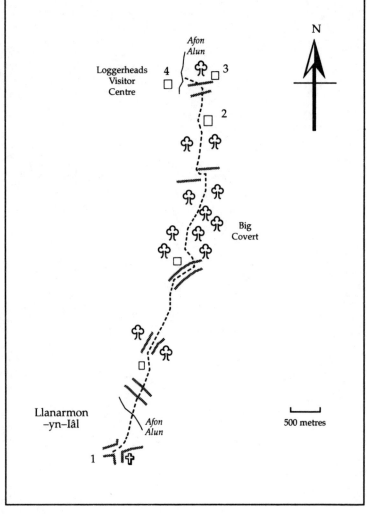

Loggerheads Visitor Centre

Afon Alun

Big Covert

Llanarmon –yn–Iâl

Afon Alun

N

500 metres

Llanarmon-yn-Iâl – Big Covert – Loggerheads

Route:	Moderate. Field and woodland paths. Some climbing.
Time:	3-3½ hours.
Start:	Bus stop in Llanarmon-yn-Iâl. GR 189561.
Finish:	Loggerheads Country Park Visitor Centre. GR 198626.
Public Transport:	Llanarmon-yn-Iâl and Loggerheads are both on the B5 Yr Wyddgrug-Rhuthun (Mold-Ruthin) bus route, but note that not all buses call at both places. Buses from Chester, Y Fflint and Wrecsam to Yr Wyddgrug (Mold). Buses from Rhyl and Corwen to Rhuthun. From late May to late September Llanarmon-yn-Iâl and the Loggerheads Country Park are linked by the Clwydian Ranger Bus (Red Line).
Parking:	On street parking near the bus stop in Llanarmon-yn-Iâl. Car park at Loggerheads Visitor Centre. Alternatively park in Yr Wyddgrug or Rhuthun, and catch a bus to the start and from the finish.
Facilities:	Pub and shop in Llanarmon-yn-Iâl. Cafe and toilets at Loggerheads Visitor Centre. Pub nearby.
OS Maps:	1:50 000 Landranger 116 and 117; 1:25 000 Explorer 265.

Points of Interest:

1. Llanarmon-yn-Iâl is set amidst attractive, hilly countryside on the east side of the Clwydian range. In the large churchyard

stands the church dedicated to St Garmon, also known as Germanus and, until Tudor times, it was a place of pilgrimage. The church has several medieval features including a timber roof, and a brass chandelier that was made in Bruges about 500 years ago. There is an effigy of the knight Gruffudd ap Llywelyn ap Ynyr (c.1320), and one of a 14th century priest. On the wall is a mural to Captain Efan Llwyd who died in the early 17th century. The church was restored in the 1730s, and the windows, font and wooden pillars separating the church belong to this period. Before starting your walk, you may like to follow the road downhill to Afon Alun. On the far side of the river is Tomen y Faerdre, an impressive 11th century motte on a rocky outcrop that was probably the home of local rulers. It was refortified by King John in 1212 during his campaign against Llywelyn ab Iorwerth. On the other side of the lane is a large cave, where prehistoric remains have been found. Nearby is the farmhouse known as Plas Isaf, which was part of the medieval manor house.

2. The Outdoor Centre at Colomendy was planned and built as one of several national camp schools to be used in wartime. Children evacuated from Liverpool during the blitz came here in 1939. Since *Liverpool Corporation* bought Colomendy in 1956, it has become an environmental studies centre.

3. The Boundary Stone is known as *Carreg Carn March Arthur*, because it is indented with a mark similar to horses' hoof print. It is said to have been made by King Arthur's horse after leaping from Moel Fama. The stone above it was erected in 1763, to settle a prolonged dispute over mining rights. It marks the boundary between the lordships of Yr Wyddgrug in Flintshire and Llanferres in Denbighshire. The dispute inspired the artist Richard Wilson to paint the original sign for *We Three Loggerheads Inn*. The sign is of two men, back to back, looking in opposite directions. The third loggerhead (meaning 'blockhead') is the person looking at it. The area's name,

Loggerheads, originated from the sign.

4. The site where Loggerheads Visitor Centre is now, was bought in 1926 by the *Crosville* bus company and for many years buses carried thousands of visitors from Merseyside to this beauty spot. The local council bought the land in 1974, and it is now a country park. To read more about Loggerheads see Walk 5, Point of Interest 4.

Walk Directions: (–) denotes Point of Interest

1. From the bus stop in Llanarmon-yn-Iâl (1), follow the road to the church. At the church gates, turn left to pass *The Raven Inn* on your right. In a few metres, turn right on a track between buildings and take a path to a stile, then turn left over another.

2. Walk ahead through the field and descend the hill by slanting right to a stile. Go through the middle of the field to another stile, then walk beside a left-hand hedge to a corner stile. Turn right downhill and, at the bottom of the field, bear left along the boundary. Cross a stile and footbridge over Afon Alun. Go through a kissing gate to emerge onto a track giving access to a caravan site. Turn left on an enclosed path and follow it to a road.

3. Cross the road to a track and pass houses on the left. Go through a gate and walk along a track bordered by trees. Pass through another gate across the track and ignore a permissive path on the left. With a quarry on your left, continue along the bridleway. Maintain your direction and, at Bryn-y-gloch, follow a path and drive to a lane.

4. Turn right and ignore a track on the left and a stile on the right. Go through a gate at the end of the lane and walk ahead on a clear track to have a limestone hill on your right. Go downhill and veer slightly right to a hidden gate near trees. Turn left on the earth track.

5. After about 50 metres, cross a stile on the right and bear left. The path soon bears right beside a fence. Climb a ladder stile and follow the fence to a stile and lane. Turn right and pass Bryn yr Orsedd on the left. In another 200 metres, after passing houses on the left, turn left onto a track and, in about 40 metres, bear right onto a footpath.

6. Go uphill through deciduous trees and ignore a path on the left and another on the right. Pass an area of cleared forest. Stay on the main track and ignore other tracks and paths leading off. Descend to a stile at a gate and turn right onto a track to a road.

7. Turn left and walk downhill. When the lane goes left downhill, keep ahead (right) on a level track. Ignore a track on the right but, in about another 80 metres, go right uphill onto another track to pass Bryn Tirion Cottage.

8. Go through a gate at the end of the track and continue on a path. Walk through scrub and trees to a stile and continue through woodlands. Go downhill to a group of stiles and bear right. Reach a lane at an Outdoor Centre (2), and walk ahead for a few metres then bear left. Ignore a left turning (a No Through Road) and, at a fork, go right. Go right again to pass buildings on the left. Continue on a track downhill through the woods.

9. Emerge on the A494 and cross the road to the Boundary Stone (3). Go through gates and walk ahead along a broad track. At a fork, go left and descend to a bridge over Afon Alun. Cross to reach the Loggerheads Visitor Centre (4) and car park. Nearby, on the A494, are bus stops and the inn named *We Three Loggerheads*.

WALK 8

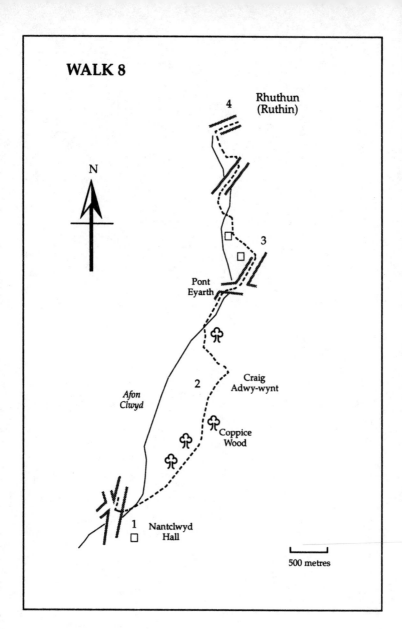

Rhuthun
(Ruthin)

4

N

3

Pont
Eyarth

Craig
Adwy-wynt

2

*Afon
Clwyd*

Coppice
Wood

1 Nantclwyd
Hall

500 metres

Nantclwyd Hall – Craig Adwy-wynt – Pont Eyarth – Rhuthun (Ruthin)

Route:	Moderate. Gradual climb to a limestone ridge above Afon Clwyd. Field and woodland paths.
Time:	3-4 hours.
Start:	On the A494, at the turn-off for Clocaenog, near the bridge over Afon Clwyd. GR 109519.
Finish:	St Peter's Square, Rhuthun. GR 122582.
Public Transport:	Buses 151 and 152 from Rhyl or Rhuthun to Wrecsam or Corwen go along the A494. Ask for the Clocaenog turn-off, roughly 2 miles south of Pwllglas, near the bridge over Afon Clwyd.
Parking:	Bottom of Clwyd Street, Rhuthun.
Facilities:	None on the route. Full facilities in Rhuthun.
OS Maps:	1:50 000 Landranger 116; 1:25 000 Explorer 256.

Points of Interest:

1. The present Nantclwyd Hall dates from the 17th century, but the mansion was altered and extended in the 18th and 19th centuries. In the mid 20th century, it was elaborately remodelled by the Welsh architect Sir Clough Williams-Ellis, who designed the famous Italianate village, Portmeirion.

2. Craig Adwy-wynt is a limestone escarpment known for its wild flowers and butterflies. From the ridge are wide views over the Vale of Clwyd and to the Clwydian hills. Look and listen for stonechat, yellowhammer and meadow pipit. On the descent, you pass the site of an Iron Age hillfort.

3. Eyarth Station was a halt on the branch line of the *London and North Western Railway* between Rhyl, Dinbych, Rhuthun and Corwen. It opened in 1864, but closed in the 1960's. The station is now a guest house.

4. With buildings spanning over seven hundred years of history, Rhuthun is an attractive market town built on rising ground above Afon Clwyd. The present castle is a 19th century mansion, which incorporates remains of the medieval fortress. It is now a luxury hotel. The original castle stood against the attack by Owain Glyndŵr in 1400, but, two days later, Lord Grey of Rhuthun was captured when away from his stronghold, and had to pay 10,000 marks for his release. During the Civil War, the castle was eventually lost, in 1666, to the Parliamentarians. Rhuthun has many listed buildings. St Peter's Church, north of the square, was founded in 1310, and has a splendid carved oak roof. The gates to the churchyard were designed by the famous Davies Brothers of Bersham.

Walk Directions: (–) denotes Point of Interest

1. On the A494, walk in the direction of Bala and, in a few metres, before reaching Afon Clwyd, cross a ladder stile on the left. Emerge onto an old road and follow a path through the trees. Cross Nantclwyd drive (1) and go ahead to a gate. Walk on with the river on your right.

2. Cross an ornamental bridge over the river and head diagonally left across parkland. Go through a gate and walk uphill, slightly left, through scattered trees. Pass a copse on your left and walk on with a wood on your right. At a second copse on your left, go through a bridle gate on your right into the wood.

3. Follow a narrow path that slants left through the trees. It becomes wider and goes up to a gate. Walk on to reach a track and continue ahead to a gate (ignore a gate on the right into a

field). Follow a right-hand fence to another gate, but don't go through it. Bear left across a field and pass a large tree.

4. Ignore a gate below on the left but go ahead to another gate. Walk ahead on a path and pass a corner fence on the right. In about another 40 metres, at a fork, go left on a slighter path. Continue through Coppice Wood and pass ruined cottages. Go ahead through a gap and cross a stile near a corrugated iron building.

5. Go ahead slightly right up to a stile but, if this route is impassable, take the left-hand path which leads to a gate. Continue uphill through bracken and take a path onto the limestone ridge (2).

6. Continue ahead along the ridge, passing broken fences. Go slightly right on a path for a few paces, then left on a clear path that curves to the right through bracken. Go through a gate and walk on between trees until you meet another gate. Do not go through, but bear left on a path.

7. On reaching a wall, keep it on your right and pass above a bungalow. Ignore another path on the left and arrive at a stile. Cross to another and walk on through a field. Climb a stile on the left and walk downhill through a wood. After about 50 metres, at a corner, the path bears left. At this point, take another path on your right.

8. Have a rough field on your left, and walk downhill between fences. Pass through some trees and bear left towards houses. Go right on a clear path below the A494. This was the trackbed of the former Corwen-Rhyl railway.

9. Emerge at a road junction on the A494 and bear right. Cross Pont Eyarth and, after another 200 metres, go left on another lane. Pass Eyarth Old Railway Station (3) on the left and, at the end of the gardens, go left through a small gate and cross a stile.

10. Slant right to a stile and cross the field to another. Go through a narrow field to the next stile. Walk beside the left-hand field boundary and ignore a gate on the left. Pass some trees and a pond on the right and continue beside the left-hand fence as it slants left to a gate. Walk towards a farm and go through a gate. Head towards the right-hand side of the farm and pass through a gate onto the farm drive.

11. Follow the farm drive and cross a bridge over the river. Climb a stile on the right and slant left to a gate in the top corner. Emerge onto a road and turn right. After 700 metres, just before the drive to Scott House, cross a stile on the left.

12. Walk along the right side of the field and go through a kissing gate. Pass through a tunnel and cross a stile. Continue to a picnic and recreational area near Afon Clwyd. Walk through a car park to a road and turn right to St Peter's Square in the centre of Rhuthun (4).

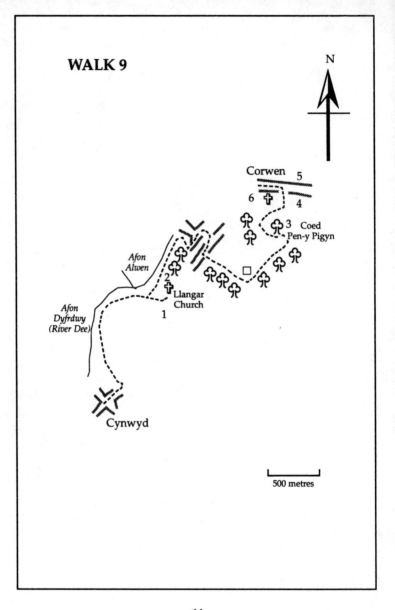

WALK 9

N

Corwen

5

6

4

Coed
Pen-y Pigyn

3

*Afon
Alwen*

*Afon
Dyfrdwy
(River Dee)*

2

Llangar
Church

1

Cynwyd

500 metres

Cynwyd – Llangar church
– Coed Pen-y-pigyn – Corwen

Route:	Easy-Moderate. Level walking along riverside field paths and an old trackbed followed by a climb on woodland paths and tracks to a fine viewpoint over Corwen.
Time:	2-3 hours.
Start:	Bus stop in centre of Cynwyd. GR 056411.
Finish:	Corwen Square. GR 079434.
Public Transport:	Bus no. 94 Wrecsam-Abermaw (Barmouth) links Cynwyd with Corwen. Corwen is also on bus route no. 70 Llandudno-Llanrwst-Wrecsam and no. 152 Dinbych (Denbigh)-Llangollen.
Parking:	Car park 100 metres from the Square in Corwen.
Facilities:	Pubs in Cynwyd. Pubs and cafes in Corwen. Public toilets in Corwen car park.
OS Maps:	1:50 000 Landranger 125; 1:25 000 Explorer 255.

Points of Interest:

1. Llangar church lies on sloping ground in a beautiful setting above the confluence of the Alwen and Dyfrdwy (Dee) rivers. This medieval church was abandoned in the late 19th century after a new parish church was built in Cynwyd. In 1967, it was taken into state care, and since then has been restored. The interior contains a series of wall paintings of at least eight different dates between the 14th century and the mid 18th century. Access to the church is by prior arrangement with the custodian of Rug chapel. If you walk around the brightly

whitewashed exterior walls, you will see, in the SE corner, a stone with the initials EM and the date 1617. Around the corner of the church are the tombstones of the Reverend Edward Samuel (1674-1748) and his son. Both were rectors of Llangar church.

2. The railway line was part of the Rhiwabon (Ruabon) to Abermaw (Barmouth) line which connected the NW of England with the Cambrian Coast at Morfa Mawddach. Opened in 1866, it was closed in the 1960s. The trackbed is now managed as a nature reserve and provides an important habitat for birds, mammals and wild flowers.

3. The monument on Pen-y-pigyn was built in 1863 by local people to commemorate the marriage of the Prince of Wales (the later Edward VII) to Princess Alexander of Denmark. It was restored in 1911 for the investiture of their son at Caernarfon castle. From here are fine views of Corwen below and Caer Drewyn, an Iron Age hillfort, on the opposite side of the valley. It is thought that Caer Drewyn may have been the headquarters of Owain Gwynedd in 1165, before his troops defeated Henry II's army at the Battle of Crogen, in the Ceiriog Valley.

4. Corwen Manor was originally a union workhouse. It was built in 1840 to house paupers from the surrounding parishes. There were separate wings for men and women. Behind the workhouse is a small quarry, where the inmates earned their keep by breaking up stones for roads.

5. Corwen straddles Thomas Telford's London to Caergybi (Holyhead) road. Until recent times, this was a busy market town and halting place for cattle drovers and stage coach travellers. George Borrow stayed at the *Owain Glyndŵr Inn*. In 1789, the first eisteddfod, into which the general public was admitted, was held here. A statue of Owain Glyndŵr is in the Square.

6. Corwen Parish church is dedicated to St Mael and St Sulien, the two missionaries from Brittany, who founded a religious community here in the 6th century. In the churchyard, to your left near the lychgate, are low gravestones with grooves for kneeling. Behind the church is the shaft of a cross which is similar to Eliseg's Pillar at Llangollen. It is set in a flat stone with artificial depressions, which may be cup marks. These are rare in Wales. At the back of the churchyard, Corwen College was established in 1750 as six almshouses for the widows of clergymen. The stone forming a lintel above the south door of the church has a mark that looks like a dagger. According to local legend, it was formed by Owain Glyndŵr's dagger when, in a fit of rage, he flung it from Pen-y-pigyn, the hill behind the church. It was probably a Celtic cross. Built into the entrance porch of the north door is a prehistoric stone. The interior of the 13th century church has some interesting features, including a Norman font and a medieval dug-out chest.

Walk Directions: (–) denotes Point of Interest

1. From the bus stop in Cynwyd, follow the road in the direction of Corwen. Pass the parish church and, in another 100 metres, turn left on an enclosed footpath. At the end of the path, cross a stile into a field and continue beside a broken left-hand hedge. Cross a stile beside a gate onto the old railway trackbed.

2. Turn right for a few paces, then go left through a field gate. Walk ahead, slightly right, to the bank of Afon Dyfrdwy (River Dee) and continue through fields with the river on your left. Pass the remains of a footbridge at a bend in the river and reach a stile opposite the confluence of Afon Alwen and Afon Dyfrdwy.

3. Walk ahead, slightly right, and go through a gap into another field, then walk up to a stile and gate. Cross the old railway trackbed to a kissing gate and follow a track to a left-hand gate signed Eglwys Llangar Church. A path goes through

the field to the church (1).

4. Return to the railway trackbed (2) and turn right. The track passes through deciduous woodland beside Afon Dyfrdwy. When it ends at a stile, walk ahead through a large garden and, further on, have a fence on your left. Cross a stile in the left-hand corner and continue ahead on a track. Follow it around to the right and, as it rises to a road, take a path on the left to a stile.

5. Emerge at the junction of the B4401 with the A5. Go right for a few metres, then cross the B4401 with care and turn left to where the road meets the A5. Immediately, bear right uphill on a partly stepped path through woods to a road.

6. Turn right and, in about 150 metres, before the road descends more steeply, turn left on an enclosed path. Pass between gardens, then walls, and go through a small gate across the path. Ignore a permissive path on the left and continue uphill on a path through trees and bracken.

7. Pass through a small gate and walk ahead to a track. Pass a house on the left and continue to a track junction in an area of recently felled forest.

8. Turn left and stay on the main track. Cross a bridge over a stream and, in another 250 metres, go left on a track at a footpath signpost. Pass through a gate and shortly take a path on the left to a memorial at Pen-y-pigyn (3).

9. With your back to the memorial and viewpoint, take a clear path on the right through the woods. It follows a wall around to the left. In about another 200 metres, the path veers right away from the wall, to a path junction at a footpath signpost. Nearby is the Gorsedd stone circle, which was built in 1919 for the opening of the National Victory Eisteddfod held in Corwen.

10. Turn right downhill and, in about 100 metres, bear right at a fork in the path. Continue through woodlands and pass behind

Corwen church and some gardens. On leaving the woods, go left to the A5. On your right is Corwen Manor (4).

11. Bear left to Corwen Square (5). To visit the church, pass the *Owain Glyndŵr Hotel* and turn left through the lychgate (6).

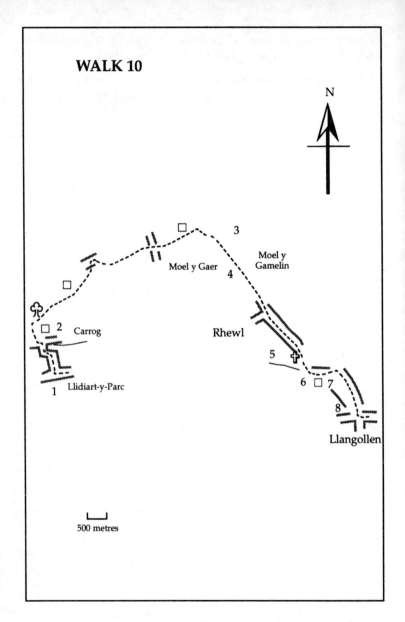

WALK 10

N

3

Moel y Gamelin

Moel y Gaer

4

Rhewl

Carrog

5

2

6 7

Llidiart-y-Parc

8

1

Llangollen

500 metres

Llidiart-y-parc – Carrog – Nant-y-madwen – Tan-y-foel – Rhewl – Llangollen

Route:	Moderate-Strenuous. Gradual climbs and fairly level walking through moorland, with an easy finish beside the Llangollen Canal.
Time:	About 5½ hours.
Start:	Bus stop at Llidiart-y-parc. GR 119433.
Finish:	Bridge over Afon Dyfrdwy (River Dee), Llangollen. GR 214421.
Public Transport:	Llidiart-y-parc and Llangollen are on the Wrecsam-Abermaw (Barmouth) no. 94 bus route. Trains to Wrecsam. Bus nos. 555/X5/5 Wrecsam-Llangollen. Seasonal trains on the Llangollen Railway from Llangollen to Carrog.
Parking:	Roadside south side of Pont Carrog. Car parks in Llangollen.
Facilities:	Pub in Carrog. Pub 600m off-route at Rhewl. Public toilets and picnic area slightly off-route in car park at Llantysilio Common. Full facilities in Llangollen.
OS Maps:	1:50 000 Landranger 125; 116 and 117. 1:25 000 Explorer 256.

Points of Interest:

1. About a kilometre east of Llidiart-y-parc is a tree covered motte known as Owain Glyndŵr's Mound. It may originally have been the site of a Norman castle, but later it was part of the Glyndyfrdwy estate, the ancestral home of Owain Glyndŵr, whose moated mansion stood in the adjacent field. The

building was destroyed by the English in 1403. Traditionally, it is believed that Owain Glyndŵr was declared Prince of Wales on the mound in September 1400, at the start of the rebellion against English rule.

2. Carrog used to be called Llansantffraid Glyndyfrdwy until the railway arrived in the 1860s, and then the name of the hamlet was changed to Carrog (the name of a nearby farm) to make it easier for tourists to pronounce. The village expanded as wealthy Victorian and Edwardian families from Merseyside built holiday homes beside the river. It is said that Owain Glyndŵr imprisoned his enemies in a house called Carchardy, that once stood in the village.

3. Plas yn Yale was the ancestral home of the Yale family who took the name of the district (Iâl) where they lived. There is a Yale chapel in Bryneglwys church. The family emigrated to America in 1637 and Elihu Yale was born there in 1649. They returned to Britain when he was four years old, and he later joined the *East India Company*. After making a fortune in India, he provided funds for the foundation of a college in America. In gratitude for his help, the college was named after him.

4. Moel y Gamelin, at 1896 feet (577m), is the highest summit on Llantysilio Mountain, the name given to the range of hills that stretches from the Horseshoe Pass to Carrog. On the summit is a 4000 year old tumulus. The hill offers spectacular views of Eglwyseg Mountain, the Clwydian range, Y Berwyn and, on a clear day, peaks of Eryri (Snowdonia). On Moel y Gaer is an Iron Age hill fort dating from about 600BC.

5. Llantysilio church is dedicated to St Tysilio, who was the son of Brochwel Ysgythrog, a Prince of Powys in the 7th century. Dating from the 15th century, the building has some medieval features, including the oak roof, lectern and 15th century glass. The church is usually open on weekend afternoons during the summer.

6. Thomas Telford constructed the Horseshoe Falls in the early 19th century, to feed water from Afon Dyfrdwy (River Dee) into the Llangollen Canal. The canal was built to form a link with the north Wales coalfield and the Dee, Mersey and Severn rivers. Slate, coal, limestone and agricultural products were carried along it until trade declined with the increasing use of road and rail transport in the early 20th century. During the summer, you will probably meet horse-drawn barges as you walk along the towpath to Llangollen.

7. *Chain Bridge Hotel* is named after the footbridge spanning Afon Dyfrdwy. It was built in 1929 to replace one built in 1870, that was destroyed by floods. The first footbridge here was erected in 1814 to carry coal to the main road for delivery in Corwen and other local towns and villages.

8. One of the 'Seven Wonders of Wales', Llangollen Bridge dates from 1346, when it was founded by John Trefor, Bishop of Llanelwy (St Asaph). The structure has been repaired and altered many times, and an additional arch was built in the 1860s for the railway to pass underneath it.

Walk Directions: (–) denotes Point of Interest

1. From the A5 in Llidiart-y-parc (1), take the lane in the direction of Carrog (2). Cross the 17th century bridge spanning Afon Dyfrdwy (River Dee), and turn left. Immediately after passing the *Grouse Inn*, turn right. Follow a path uphill. It turns left, then right, to a stile.

2. Walk on beside a right-hand fence and cross a stile at the top of the woods. Continue beside the fence, but when it starts to go downhill, go left to a stile. Slant slightly right uphill through the middle of the field to a stile near gates. Continue with a broken wall on the left to a stone stile beside a gate.

3. Follow a track between fences and hedges. Pass ruins on the

right and a house some distance to the left. After a stile, walk on beside a right-hand fence through two fields to a stile. Have a fence on the left and, when it bends left, continue ahead. Gradually descend the field to a stile and gate in the far corner.

4. Turn right for 50 metres and opposite a lane on the left, go through a gate on the right. Walk uphill on a grassy track for about 350 metres then leave it to follow a banking on the left. Follow it to the left around a corner then slant right to a gate. Go through it and veer left. Follow a fence on your left.

5. Walk along a clear path to a gate and continue below moorland. Further on have a wall on your left. After going through another gate, you will have fine views of Llantysilio Mountain. Walk on beside a left-hand fence and go downhill to cross a stream.

6. Cross a lane near a cattle grid and continue beside a fence. Ignore a stile on the left and walk on to a stile at a gate. Continue on an overgrown track and go through a gate then follow a left-hand fence to a stile. Pass behind a farm and cross a stile. Continue beside the fence and go downhill to cross a stream. Climb two more stiles and join a track.

7. Walk ahead but, after about 20 metres, go right, uphill, on a waymarked path. After 50 metres, slant left to a stile next to a gate in the top fence. Continue, slanting left, to another stile and a grassy track. Turn right and go through a gate across the track. Follow the clear track through heather and bracken. From here are fine views of the Clwydian hills and in the woods to the left is Plas yn Yale (3).

8. Climb to the pass between Moel y Gamelin and Moel y Gaer (4). Walk on downhill with fine views of the Dee Valley. Ignore paths leading off and continue downhill to a stile at a gate. Join a lane and descend to a junction.

9. Turn left and pass houses, a school and Llantysilio Farm. Go

on downhill and pass the entrance gates to Llantysilio Hall. At Llantysilio church (5) bear right and go through a kissing gate near the lychgate. Follow a path that descends and bears left to a kissing gate. Walk on beside Afon Dyfrdwy and go through another gate. Continue through the field to the Horseshoe Falls (6).

10. Go through a gate and walk on beside the Llangollen Canal. Go under a road bridge and pass behind the *Chain Bridge Hotel* (7). Continue with the canal on your left. Follow the towpath under a bridge. Further on, you will see the International Eisteddfod Pavilion on your right. At Llangollen Wharf, go right to Abbey Road. The bus stops are near the bridge (8). Another bus stop for Wrecsam is in Market Street.

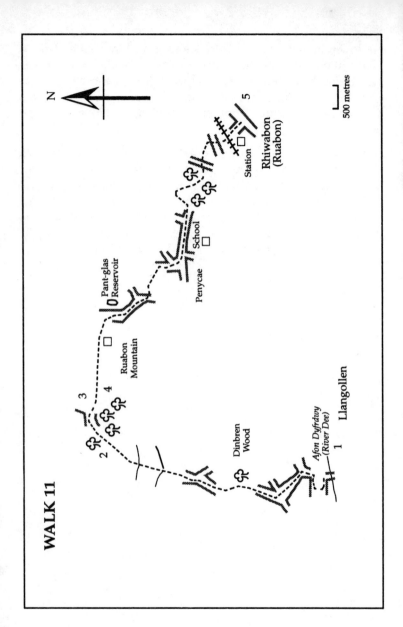

WALK 11

N

500 metres

Rhiwabon
(Ruabon)

5

Station

School

Penycae

Pant-glas
Reservoir

Ruabon
Mountain

3

4

2

Dinbren
Wood

Afon Dyfrdwy
(River Dee)

1

Llangollen

76

Llangollen – Dinbren Wood
– Mynydd Rhiwabon (Ruabon Mountain)
– Pen-y-cae – Rhiwabon (Ruabon)

Route:	Strenuous, woodlands, scree path, moorland, tracks and lanes.
Time:	About 6 hours.
Start:	Bridge over Afon Dyfrdwy (River Dee), Llangollen. GR 214421.
Finish:	Rhiwabon (Ruabon) Railway Station, GR 300438 or bus stops on the B5605 nearby. GR 301437.
Public Transport:	Bus no. 94 Wrecsam-Abermaw (Barmouth) and Bus nos. 555/X5/5 Wrecsam-Llangollen link Rhiwabon Station and Llangollen. Rhiwabon is on the Shrewsbury-Chester Railway Line.
Parking:	Car parks at Rhiwabon Railway Station and in Llangollen.
Facilities:	Full facilities in Llangollen. Pubs in Pen-y-cae and Rhiwabon.
OS Maps:	1:50 000 Landranger 117.
	1:25 000 Explorer 256.

Points of Interest:

1. Llangollen is famous throughout the world for its International Music Eisteddfod, which takes place every year in July. The town's name comes from a Celtic saint called Collen, who had been a hermit in Glastonbury. He eventually came to the Vale of Llangollen to live in a cave by the river, and he built a church nearby. One of the many legends about him relates

how he rid Llangollen of a terrifying giantess who ate travellers. By the 19th century, many visitors were visiting Llangollen and it was an important staging post on the London to Caergybi (Holyhead) road. The town was also well known for its flannel.

2. Plas Uchaf is an Elizabethan half-timbered manor house which, according to local legend, was built on the site of a hunting lodge owned by Cadwgan, Prince of Powys. His son, Owain, raided Pembroke castle in 1108 and kidnapped Nest, the wife of the Norman lord Gerald of Pembroke. It is said he brought her to this valley and hid her in the hunting lodge, from where she was eventually returned. During the Civil War, Colonel John Jones, brother-in-law of Oliver Cromwell, lived in the manor house. He was a signatory to the death warrant of Charles I, and was executed on the Restoration of the monarchy.

3. The towering crag at World's End is called Craig y Forwyn (Maiden's Crag). It is thought the name refers to the story of a young girl in love, who jumped to her death from the rock. The crag is popular with climbers.

4. The cross is in memory of the pilot who died in World War Two when his Bristol Beaufighter crashed in poor visibility on the moorland. During the war, over a dozen aircraft were lost on the 1649 foot mountain. These included several Spitfires. The pilot of an Airspeed Oxford was killed in 1944, when his aircraft hit a pine tree above World's End. Decoy lights were set up on the mountain to simulate built up areas and craters can still be seen from the jettisoned German bombs. For nearly fifty years afterwards, unexploded bombs were found on the moorland. The mountain is now a conservation area. From the highest point on the route are extensive views over the Cheshire and Shropshire Plains.

5. Bronze and Iron Age finds around Rhiwabon indicate that

the place has been a settlement since early times. In the area are the two great 8th century earthworks known as Wat's Dyke and Offa's Dyke. The present church of St Mary was established by the monks of Valle Crucis Abbey. In the church are memorials to the wealthy Williams-Wynn family of Wynnstay Hall. The mansion was sold to Lindisfarne College in 1950. During the industrial revolution, Rhiwabon developed rapidly, as the area was rich in mineral deposits. Coal mines and iron works were established. Rich deposits of clay lead to the opening of brick and terracotta works. Nowadays, few works remain from Rhiwabon's industrial past, and most people commute elsewhere.

Walk Directions: (–) denotes Point of Interest

1. From Llangollen (1) cross the bridge and walk up to the A542. Cross and turn left but, in a few metres, take a path on the right up to the canal. Turn right, then left to cross a bridge over the canal. Immediately, turn left along Dinbren Road.

2. Ignore lanes leading off to the right and left. After just over a kilometre, ignore a footpath on the right into a field. After about another 50 metres, cross a stile on the right and follow a clear path through trees. Go over a track and cross a stile then continue on a path through woodlands to another stile. After a few metres, bear right on a path and cross a small footbridge on the left. Bear right through the field and some trees to a ladder stile and lane.

3. Turn right to a lane junction below the Eglwyseg crags and bear left. In about 800 metres, leave the lane for a footpath on the right. It has an acorn sign, the waymark of the Offa's Dyke long distance path. Go through a gate and follow the track to a gate at a house. Continue beside a fence but, in about 50 metres, leave it at a corner and continue on a clear path below the limestone escarpment.

4. In places, the path is quite narrow. It descends to a fence beside trees. At a corner, leave the fence to take a path that crosses a stream and goes above a wood. Pass another corner fence and follow a narrow path above woodlands, below crags and over a stream. Continue on a path across the screes and, at a fork, go left. After about 600 metres climb a ladder stile and pass above Plas Uchaf Manor House (2).

5. Cross another stile and pass through an area of felled forest to a stile and lane. Turn right but, in a few paces and before the lane bends left over a ford, cross a stile on the right. Walk uphill on a path. As the path climbs higher, it becomes rougher and passes Craig y Forwyn (3). Keep on uphill to a stile.

6. Walk ahead, slightly left, to a track. If you are at the right spot, there should be a waymarked path almost opposite. Follow the path through heather and bracken to a fork. Go left to a path junction and walk ahead through heather. You should pass a few waymarks. At a flat area, ignore paths leading off but, as you start to descend, look on the right for stones in the shape of a cross (4).

7. Continue along the footpath and ignore a path on the right that goes to Mountain Lodge. Cross over a track and continue ahead. Follow a track to a gate and walk up to a lane.

8. Turn right on the lane and pass Pant-glas reservoir on the left. Go left at a bend and ignore a bridleway on the right. Follow the lane downhill. Pass houses and ignore footpaths on the left and right.

9. At a fork, take the right-hand lane and, in about 300 metres, at a right bend, bear left onto a track. This was once part of the old road between Llandegla and Rhiwbon. After about 600 metres, at the second left bend, climb a stile on your right and follow the left boundary of fields, parallel to the track, to a stile. Rejoin the track and walk ahead to a road.

10. Turn right and walk downhill. Cross a bridge and, at a road junction, turn left in the direction of Rhiwabon.

11. Pass a school on the right and follow the road downhill. Ignore a road on the left but, in about another 100 metres, go left onto a track. Go over a footbridge and cross a playing field. Walk uphill on a clear path and follow it around to the right and into a field. Go slightly right to another field and continue on a path that descends above trees.

12. The path reaches the corner of woodlands. Continue on a clear path with a stream on the right. Ignore paths leading off and stay on the main path. Ignore a footbridge on the right and walk on through the woods. Emerge onto a drive and go ahead to a lane.

13. Cross the lane slightly right and go up steps to a footpath. Pass through a kissing gate and follow the left-hand hedge to a stile. Continue along a path to a road.

14. Turn right for about 30 metres then bear left on a path that passes between houses. Go over a footbridge and through a tunnel below the railway line. The path rises to the car park at Rhiwabon Station. Turn right to the station. Bus stops nearby and in Rhiwabon (5).

WALK 12

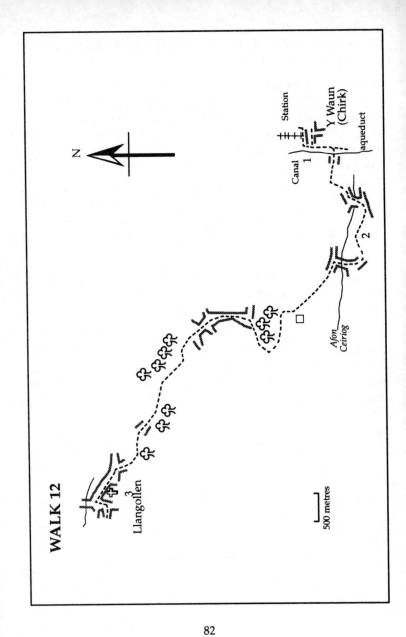

N

Station

Y Waun
(Chirk)

aqueduct

Canal
1

2

Afon
Ceiriog

Llangollen

3

500 metres

Y Waun (Chirk) – Afon Ceiriog
– Llwybr Ceiriog Trail – Llangollen

Route: Moderate-Strenuous. Field, riverside, canal
                    and woodland paths, tracks and lanes.
Time: About 5 hours.
Start: Y Waun (Chirk) Railway Station. GR 284378.
Finish: Llangollen, Market Street. GR 213420.
Public Transport: Y Waun is on the Chester-Wrecsam-
                    Shrewsbury Railway Line. Buses no. 5A
                    Wrecsam-Llangollen-Y Waun (town), no. 22
                    Wrecsam-Rhiwabon-Y Waun (town)-
                    Llangollen and no. 64 Llangollen-Y Waun
                    (station)-Glyn Ceiriog link Y Waun and
                    Llangollen. There is also Bus no. 2 Wrecsam-
                    Oswestry to Y Waun (town). Y Waun station
                    is served by Bus no. 65 Wrecsam-Llanarmon
                    D.C. Buses serving Llangollen include Bus no.
                    94 Abermaw (Barmouth)-Wrecsam and Bus
                    nos. 5/5X/555 Wrecsam-Llangollen.
Parking: Y Waun (Chirk) Station and Llangollen
                    Market Street.
Facilities: Refreshments in Y Waun. Public toilets in Y
                    Waun car park (600 metres off-route). Full
                    facilities in Llangollen.
OS Maps: 1:50 000 Landranger 117 and 126;
                    1:25 000 Explorer 256.

Points of Interest:

1. The Llangollen branch of the Shropshire Union Canal was
constructed to provide a link between the Severn, Dee and
Mersey rivers but the north-east extension to Wrecsam and

Chester was never completed. The 421 foot Chirk (Y Waun) tunnel was built so that the view from Castell y Waun (Chirk castle) would not be spoilt by the canal and its barges. On the south side of the canal is the ten arched Chirk Aqueduct which stands 70 feet above Afon Ceiriog. It carries the canal from Wales to England and was built between 1796 and 1801, by Thomas Telford. Standing beside it, but 30 feet higher, is the railway viaduct that was built by Scotsman Henry Robertson between 1846 and 1848 to carry the Shrewsbury to Chester railway line.

2. Chirk castle dates from the 13th century, when Edward I gave land to Roger Mortimer. The castle was purchased for about £5,000 in 1595, by Sir Thomas Myddleton, who was a son of the governor of Denbigh castle and a founder of the *East India Company*. He added a new north range. His son, the second Sir Thomas, was a Parliamentarian and he lost the castle to the Royalists in 1643. Three years later, the Myddletons regained it and changed allegiance. In revenge, The Parliamentarians destroyed part of the castle. The Myddleton family still own much of the estate, but the castle is now in the care of the National Trust.

3. St Collen's church dates from the 13th century, but it was rebuilt in the mid 19th century. It has splendid hammerbeam roofs and a 14th century tomb. In the churchyard are buried the famous, eccentric Ladies of Llangollen. Lady Eleanor Butler and Hon. Sarah Ponsonby eloped from Ireland in the 18th century and lived together with their maid at Plas Newydd near Llangollen. They were visited by many famous people including Sir Walter Scott, Lord Byron, Wordsworth and the Duke of Wellington. Plas Newydd and its grounds can be visited by the public. To read more about Llangollen see Walk 11, Point of Interest 1.

Walk Directions: (–) denotes Point of Interest

1. From Y Waun Station, go up steps to the road and bear right. Pass the entrance to an industrial estate and, in a few metres, take a path on the right to the canal towpath. Bear left and walk through Chirk Tunnel (1).

2. On emerging from the tunnel, enjoy the views from Chirk Aqueduct then turn back in the direction of the tunnel. Before reaching it, take a path to the road. Turn left and, in about 100 metres, bear right on a path.

3. The path rises through woodlands and passes a caravan site. At the end of the site, turn left at a path junction and walk downhill to the road. Turn right and, in 100 metres, turn left and cross Pontfaen Bridge.

4. Turn right along a lane and, in about 80 metres, cross a stile on the right. Follow the grassy track ahead then pass through trees into another field. Continue beside Afon Ceiriog. Cross a stile into woodlands and ignore a path on the left. Follow a path beside the river.

5. After crossing a small footbridge, climb a stepped path. Join another path and turn left to a stile and field. From here are views of Castell y Waun (Chirk castle) (2)

6. Bear left to a stile and enclosed path. Pass through three gates and follow an access drive uphill to a road. Turn right and pass lime kilns on the left. Bear right on a lane and walk downhill to cross a bridge over the river and emerge on the B4500 at Castle Mill.

7. Cross the road directly to a lane with a dead end sign and the Offa's Dyke Path acorn symbols. Follow the lane uphill. Ignore a track on the right and, a little further on, take the right fork.

8. In about 300 metres, you will pass Crogenwladys on the left.

Continue on a track uphill beside woodland. When the track becomes level, ignore a stile on the right (for the Offa's Dyke Path). Continue along the track to a fork. Go left downhill and join another track near a house.

9. Pass the house on your left and go uphill. Join another track and turn right. Pass a footpath on the right and follow the track uphill. Ignore a track on the right and join a lane. Turn right to a road junction.

10. Turn left uphill through woodlands. On emerging from the trees, you will have views of Mynydd Rhiwabon (Ruabon Mountain) and the Cheshire Plain. Go over a crossroad and, further on, ignore a lane on the right, but at a point where the lane you are on bends left, go through the gate ahead.

11. With a fence on your right, walk downhill along the bridleway. From the track are great views of Mynydd Rhiwabon, Castell Dinas Brân, Llantysilio Mountain and Afon Dyfrdwy (River Dee). The track passes through gates and above woodlands.

12. The track descends towards trees above Pengwern Vale. Join another track and veer right to walk downhill. Ignore a path on the right and go through a gate across the track.

13. Ignore a path on the right and emerge on a lane. Turn right and pass a youth hostel on your right. At a stile on your right, go left on a track into Pen-y-coed. Pass around a barrier and continue along the edge of the wood.

14. Cross a stile at the end of the wood and walk downhill to another stile. Continue downhill to a field and, further downhill, cross a stile to follow an enclosed path. On reaching a surfaced path, go left to a track and bear right to a road.

15. Follow the road ahead and pass a car park. On reaching the A5 in Llangollen, cross at the traffic lights and turn left. In

about 50 metres, bear right on a road and pass St Collen's church (3). Continue to another road near the bridge over Afon Dyfrdwy. On your right is a bus stop for Bala and Dolgellau. For buses to Wrecsam and Y Waun, go left then right into Market Street.

WALK 13

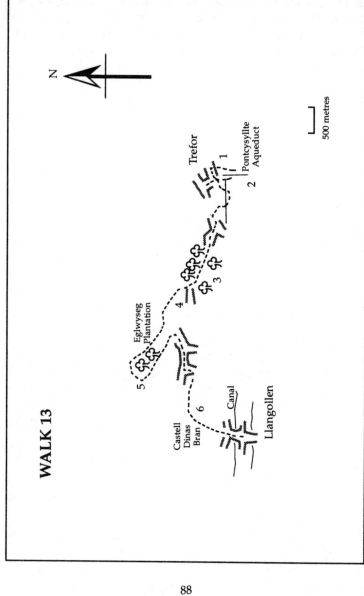

N

500 metres

Trefor

1 Pontcysyllte
2 Aqueduct

3

4

Eglwyseg
Plantation

5

Castell
Dinas
Bran

6

Canal

Llangollen

88

Trefor – Eglwyseg Plantation
– Castell Dinas Brân – Llangollen

Route:	Strenuous. Long gradual climbs from the canal towpath to moorland and hilltop are rewarded with breathtaking extensive views.
Time:	4-4½ hours.
Start:	Bus stops named Trefor Station on the A539 at the B5434 turn-off for Froncysyllte. GR 269425.
Finish:	Bridge over Afon Dyfrdwy (River Dee), Llangollen. GR 214421.
Public Transport:	Bus no. 94 Wrecsam-Abermaw (Barmouth), nos. 5/X5/555 Wrecsam-Llangollen and no. 5A Wrecsam-Y Waun (Chirk), - Llangollen link Trefor with Llangollen. Nearest railway station is Rhiwabon (Ruabon) 2½ miles from the start served by bus no. 94 and nos. 555/X5/5.
Parking:	Car parks at Trefor Wharf and in Llangollen.
Facilities:	Refreshments in Trefor and Llangollen. Public toilets at Trefor Wharf and in Llangollen.
OS Maps:	1:50 000 Landranger 117; 1:25 000 Explorer 256.

Points of Interest:

1. In the early 19th century, Trefor Wharf was linked by tramways to local collieries, quarries and ironworks. The canal was intended to be part of an ambitious waterways network, that should have extended from the River Severn to the Dee at Chester. Although the plan failed because of financial

difficulties, a branch was built to the canal's water source beyond Llangollen. It is considered one of the most scenic canals in Britain.

2. Built between 1795 and 1805, Pontcysyllte Aqueduct is the work of Thomas Telford. The cost of building this masterpiece was £47,018. Some of the 18 stone piers stand 126 feet above Afon Dyfrdwy (River Dee) and the cast iron trough is 1007 feet long. The mortar between the stones of the piers is said to contain ox blood and lime. A towpath with railings runs alongside the trough, and a walk along it is an exhilarating experience.

3. Trevor Hall was home of the Trevor family and the site, once known at Llys Trefor, dates back to medieval times. Another family home was Brynkinallt, near Y Waun (Chirk). Sir John Trevor (1637-1717) became a lawyer in London and was knighted in 1671. He was elected MP several times but, in 1695, was dismissed from the House of Commons after accepting a bribe.

4. Isaac Daniel Hooson (1880-1948) was born in nearby Rhosllannerchrugog. He worked as a solicitor in Wrecsam and is remembered for the poems that he wrote in the Welsh language for children. On the memorial, he is described as *Cyfaill i Blant Cymru* (A friend to the children of Wales).

5. Creigiau Trefor (Trefor Rocks) and Creigiau Eglwyseg extend north as far as World's End. The limestone rocks were laid down 350 million years ago in the Carboniferous period, when much of Britain lay below a warm tropical sea. On the plateau are several Bronze Age barrows, cairns and other antiquities. From the escarpment are extensive views over Castell Dinas Brân, the Dee Valley and Llantysilio Mountain.

6. Castell Dinas Brân was built in the 1260s by the lords of

Powys, but when the Earl of Lincoln and his troops arrived in 1277, they found the castle burnt and deserted. The English garrison moved in but, later, it was returned to the Welsh lords. In 1282, after Llywelyn ap Gruffudd was killed, Edward I gave the area to John de Warenne, Earl of Surrey, but he did not repair the castle. There are several legends attached to the hill, which is also the site of an Iron Age hillfort, and it is one of the sites where King Arthur is said to have left the Holy Grail. For over a hundred years, tourists have been climbing the hill for the views and, in the 19th century, a camera obscura was housed in the ruins.

Walk Directions: (–) denotes Point of Interest

1. From the bus stop, take the B5434 (Station Road) and follow it downhill. Just before *Telford's Inn* turn left and cross a bridge over the canal. Bear right into the car park and walk out to Trefor Wharf (1). Turn left alongside it to a footpath on the left. Continue a few metres if you would like a view of Pontcysyllte Aqueduct (2) or to walk a short distance along it.

2. Descend the footpath into trees. Ignore other paths on the left and follow a path under the aqueduct and up to a road. Turn right and, after crossing a bridge, bear left on a path to have the canal on your left. Cross a footbridge over the canal and continue beside it. Ignore a path on the left.

3. Cross the next footbridge then walk across a field diagonally left to a stile. Go left beside a fence and bear right with the path under an old railway line. Turn right and, at a corner, go left along an enclosed path to the road. Cross with care and bear left along the pavement.

4. Turn right on a lane signposted Trefor church and, in about 300 metres, bear left on a track. In a few metres, take a path on the right, it climbs through trees then becomes level as it follows an enclosed path alongside a field. Further on, the path

descends into Trefor Hall Wood (3) and reaches a fork. Take the right-hand path to a stile and lane.

5. On the other side of the lane is a small parking area with paths going uphill away from it. The walk takes the right-hand path but you may first like to visit the monument to I.D. Hooson (4). To do so, follow the left-hand path for about 100 metres. Return to the other path and walk uphill to a path junction.

6. Turn left at the footpath signpost and follow the permissive path uphill through heather. It crosses a couple of broken walls, and, further on, has a wall on the left. Continue alongside it to a footpath signpost. Do not turn right but walk on ahead and go through a broken wall. Pass two corner fences and descend a steep path to a path junction.

7. Bear right and follow the path uphill to a stile. Maintain your direction and, after passing a fence corner, climb a ladder stile on your right. Go left beside the fence and pass the remnants of a plantation then cross another stile on your left.

8. Walk downhill and cross over a path to reach a footpath signpost. Go left and soon walk along the edge of the limestone escarpment (5). From here you have fine views over Castell Dinas Brân.

9. Pass a fence corner and continue with the fence on your left. Follow the fence when it bends left away from the escarpment. It goes downhill and over a small rise to a corner fence and gate. Turn right along a track and walk downhill to the lane.

10. Turn right and ignore the first lane on the left. Bear left along the next lane, which has a cattle grid, and turn right through a kissing gate. Bear left and follow an obvious path uphill to a stile below Castell Dinas Brân. Continue uphill and through a ditch to the ruins (6).

11. Leave the ruins by a path at the opposite end of the hill. Walk downhill in the direction of Llangollen and follow the path to a kissing gate and track. Continue downhill and cross over a track.

12. Walk downhill to a kissing gate and continue downhill. Cross an access lane and follow an enclosed path to a road. Cross a bridge over the canal and go downhill to the bus stops near the bridge over the river in Llangollen.

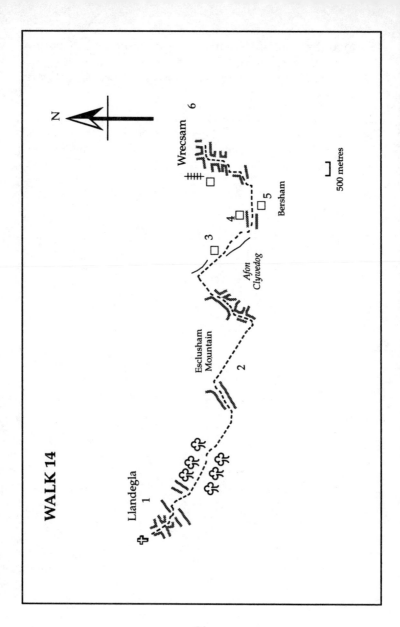

WALK 14

Llandegla

1

Esclusham
Mountain

2

3

Afon
Clywedog

4

5

Bersham

Wrecsam

6

500 metres

N

Llandegla – Esclusham Mountain
– Afon Clywedog – Wrecsam

Route:	Strenuous. Forest, moorland and riverside paths.
Time:	6-7 hours.
Start:	Bus stop in Llandegla, near the church. GR 196523
Finish:	Wrecsam bus station. GR 333505.
Public Transport:	Llandegla is on the Bus no. 158 Wrecsam-Rhuthun-Dinbych (Denbigh) bus route. Llandegla is also served by Bus no. 95 (infrequent) Melin-y-wig-Corwen-Llandegla-Wrecsam. Wrecsam is on the rail network.
Parking:	Car park near the bus stop in Llandegla. Several car parks in Wrecsam town centre.
Facilities:	Shop in Llandegla. Public toilets and picnic area at Nant Mill Visitor Centre. Full facilities in Wrecsam.
OS Maps:	1:50 000 Landranger 116 and 117; 1:25 000 Explorer 256.

Points of Interest:

1. Llandegla was a resting place for drovers taking their animals to markets in England. The village was also known for St Tegla's holy well, which was said to cure epilepsy. St Tegla was a second century female disciple of St Paul, and she lived where modern Turkey is now. She was known for her healing powers, but it is not known how her fame spread to Denbighshire. The cure involved a complex ritual, which included bathing in the well, throwing in coins and carrying a chicken (women carried a hen, men a cockerel) in a basket

around the well and churchyard. The person then slept under the communion table with the bible for a pillow. If the rites were successful, the epilepsy was transferred to the chicken. The church was rebuilt in Victorian times, but has a medieval brass chandelier and a Georgian window.

2. Heather moorland covers much of Esclusham, Rhiwabon and Eglwyseg mountains. Look out for kestrel, buzzard, sparrowhawk and peregrine falcon as well as meadow pipit and skylark. Lead was mined on the mountain in the 19th century.

3. Built in 1832 as a corn mill for the Plas Power estate, Nant Mill is now a visitor centre. The Plas Power Woods consist mainly of mature oak and beech trees and are now owned by the Woodland Trust. Sir Henry Power was Viscount of Valentia in 1620. Look out for wagtails and dipper by the river. In the 18th century, the woodland path was used for the transport of limestone from Minera to Bersham ironworks.

4. Bersham Ironworks was established in the early 18th century by Charles Lloyd. He was a Quaker, and a friend of Abraham Darby, who was the first to use coke instead of charcoal in a blast furnace. Charles Lloyd was the first to use this method in Wales in 1721. He left the Bersham Works in 1726 and, after passing through several hands, the works were acquired by Isaac Wilkinson in 1753. His two sons took over ten years later. John Wilkinson became known throughout Europe when he produced cylinders for James Watt's steam engines, and he patented a new method of boring cannon. He bought the Brymbo estate in 1792, and established iron works there. *The Bersham Works* then declined and went out of production.

5. The Bersham Heritage Centre is on the site of John Wilkinson's east works, which later became a paper mill, and was in production until the 1860s. The present building dates from 1874, and it was a school until 1961. The centre features

permanent displays about John Wilkinson's ironworks.

6. Although a modern town, Wrecsam's best known building is the church of St Giles. It is the burial place of Elihu Yale (see Walk 10, Point of Interest 3), who was a benefactor to Yale University in America. He died in 1721, and his grave is west of the tower. Built in 1506, the church steeple is one of the *Seven Wonders of Wales*. The gates to the churchyard were crafted by the Davis Brothers of Bersham, who also made Castell y Waun (Chirk castle) gates.

Walk Directions: (–) denotes Point of Interest

1. From the bus stop in Llandegla (1), follow the road past the memorial hall to the A5104. Cross the road and walk ahead along a lane. Go around a corner and descend steps on the right.

2. Cross a road and turn left. After passing some trees, cross a stile on the right. Walk ahead to a stile and, in the next field, slant left to another stile. Have a fence on the right and, in the next field, follow the left-hand hedge to a stile. Walk along a track to a lane.

3. Turn right and, at houses, turn left through a gate with an Offa's Dyke Path sign. In a few paces, bear right on a narrow path and pass a house on the left. Go uphill and through a gate. Continue along a clear path through the forest and cross a track. Go right at a fork and follow the white acorn symbols. Cross a plank bridge and more tracks. The path eventually descends to a ladder stile.

4. Follow a clear path through moorland. In places, there is a board walk to prevent erosion. Emerge onto a lane and leave the Offa's Dyke Path by turning left. In two kilometres, at a point where the lane bends left, go right on a grassy track.

5. After about 100 metres, the track bears slightly left and over

a rise. Walk on south-east through moorland (2), and in about two kilometres, you will pass a field on the left. Cross a stile near a gate and bear left in the direction of a mast. Just before reaching a gate, bear sharp right and descend to a lane.

6. Turn left and ignore a lane on the right. At a junction, turn right and walk downhill. Bear left with the lane and emerge on the B5426.

7. Turn left and take the second footpath on the right. After walking about half-way down the field, head for the far left corner. Cross into the next field and follow a right-hand hedge to a stone bridge. Continue ahead and walk downhill with trees on your right. Cross a stile and emerge on a lane.

8. Turn right, but do not cross the bridge over Afon Clywedog. Instead, bear right on the Clywedog Valley Trail and have the river on your left. Walk on through meadows and woodland. At a fork, go left beside a fence and down steps to cross a footbridge over the river. Follow a path to the Nant Mill Visitor Centre (3).

9. Pass the visitor centre on your left and walk uphill along a lane. Keep ahead at a lane junction and walk downhill. Go through a kissing gate on the left into Plas Power Woods. Follow the main path and have the river on your right.

10. The path crosses Offa's Dyke and passes a weir. Emerge on a track and at a lane, bear left to pass Bersham Ironworks (4).

11. Ignore a lane on the right and follow the lane under the A483. Walk up to another road and turn left. Ignore a road on the left and you will see the Bersham Heritage Centre (5) on your right.

12. Go through the car park and down a path. Bear left, then right, between houses. The lane becomes a track between fields. Cross a stile at a cattle grid and bear right over a bridge.

Immediately go left over a stile and along an enclosed path. Pass a garden and emerge in a field.

13. Follow the right boundary to a stile at a gate. Turn left along the lane and cross a footbridge. Immediately, turn right on a path and cross another bridge. Have the river on your left and follow a path under a road. Emerge onto a track and turn left over a footbridge.

14. Walk up to a road and, after crossing it with care, turn right. Pass a cemetery and turn left along Empress Road. Cross Bersham Road and continue along Empress Road. At its end, turn right to a junction.

15. Cross at the traffic lights and turn left. Cross a road and go right into Bellevue Park. Keep left and, on leaving the park, bear right across a road. Continue ahead over the railway bridge. At a junction, follow the sign left for the railway station, or bear right for Wrecsam (6) town centre and the bus station.

WALK 15

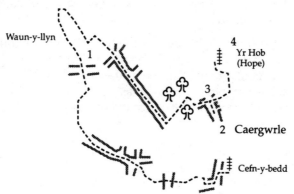

Waun-y-llyn

1

4 Yr Hob
(Hope)

3

2 Caergwrle

Cefn-y-bedd

500 metres

Cefn-y-bedd – Hope Mountain – Waun y llyn Country Park – Caergwrle – Yr Hob (Hope)

Route:	Moderate. Field, heath and woodland paths, tracks and lanes. Long gradual climb to Hope Mountain.
Time:	4 hours.
Start:	Cefn-y-bedd Railway Station. GR 310562.
Finish:	Yr Hob (Hope) Railway Station. GR 309572.
Public Transport:	Both railway stations are on the Wrecsam-Bidston (Birkenhead) line. Bus nos. 26 and 42 Wrecsam-Yr Wyddgrug (Mold) go through Cefn-y-bedd. Bus no. X23 Wrecsam-Yr Wyddgrug, limited service, passes through Cefn-y-bedd and Yr Hob.
Parking:	Cefn-y-bedd Railway Station, Caergwrle and at playing fields 500 metres from Yr Hob station.
Facilities:	Pubs en route in Caergwrle.
OS Maps:	1:50 000 Landranger 117; 1:25 000 Explorer 256.

Points of Interest:

1. Waun-y-llyn Country Park is located on the northern end of Hope Mountain. The sixty-seven acres consist mainly of grass, gorse and heather moorland, and there is a small lake. From the highest point, at 932 feet, there are extensive views across the Cheshire Plain and the Wirral Peninsula.

2. Dafydd ap Gruffudd, the brother of Llywelyn, began building Caergwrle castle in 1277. He had fought for the English against Llywelyn, and Edward I rewarded him by

giving him land and a grant to build Caergwrle castle. After the castle was built, Dafydd changed sides and on Palm Sunday, in 1282, he stormed Castell Penarlâg (Hawarden castle), starting off a new Anglo-Welsh war. Llywelyn was killed later in the year and, in 1283, Dafydd was captured and sent to Shrewsbury in chains. He was the first Welshman that was tried for treason against the English, homicide and sacrilege for which he was half-hanged, disembowelled alive and quartered. The English rebuilt Caergwrle castle and it was renamed Hope castle. Edward I gave it to his queen. Six months later, when Eleanor and Edward were staying there, a fire broke out. They escaped, but the castle was reduced to ruins and never rebuilt. In more recent times, Caergwrle enjoyed a few years as a spa on the exploitation of its sulphur and saline spring waters.

3. The packhorse bridge between Caergwrle and Yr Hob is throught to be the oldest on Afon Alun. The bridge is only four feet wide but consists of three arches with recesses. It was severely damaged by floods in November 2000, and was closed for several months whilst being repaired.

4. Yr Hob was mentioned in the *Domesday Book* and received a charter in the 14th century. Dedicated to St Cynfarch, the church dates from the 13th century with later additions. It contains effigies of the Trevor family of Plas Teg. Sir John Trevor built Plas Teg in 1610, and was elected, at separate times, MP for Flintshire and Denbighshire.

Walk Directions: (–) denotes Point of Interest

1. From the Liverpool side platform at Cefn-y-bedd Station, walk out to the A541. Cross the road with care and turn left for a few metres then turn right on the road for Brymbo. In about 50 metres, turn right on a track.

2. Ignore a path on the right and follow the track past houses. Continue to a kissing gate and follow the path uphill to some

trees. Here, take a lower path and continue to a fork in the path. Bear right uphill then veer slightly left to a stile.

3. Turn right along the lane and, in a few metres, cross a stile on the left. Veer right, passing telegraph poles, and head towards cottages. Cross a stile to the right of them and turn right on a track to a road junction. Cross directly to a lane and walk uphill. Ignore a lane on the right and in about another 1.2 kilometres, opposite a house and whilst the lane is descending, turn right onto a bridleway.

4. Follow the bridleway and ignore forks left to Tŷ Uchaf and Fron. Cross a lane to a track and pass an old farm. Stay on the track as it bends right and, at a left bend, bear right at a stile and gate into Waun-y-llyn Country Park (1).

5. Follow a path through heather and gorse and, at a fork, take the right-hand path. Pass a lake on the left and at the highest point of the path, head uphill to the viewpoint. After identifying the distant landmarks, head towards the lake, crossing two stiles. Turn right along a fence and, near the end of the field, bear left over a stile and field to emerge at a junction of lanes.

6. Take the lane directly ahead and ignore a lane on the left. Pass Sands Farm, and in about another 900 metres, cross a stile on the left.

7. Walk ahead, veering slightly left, and take a path into Bryn Yorkin Woods. On reaching a wide track, go left a few paces then turn right on a descending path. At the next track, turn left then bear right at a fork. Before reaching a fence on the right, go right downhill on another path and cross a stile. Descend the hill and climb a stile on your left and follow a road to the main road in Caergwrle.

8. The walk turns left here but, if you wish to see the castle ruins, bear right and pass *Ye Olde Castle Inn*. On the opposite

side of the road, between the post office and the memorial, a path climbs to Caergwrle castle (2).

9. Retrace your steps along the main road and, just before reaching traffic lights, turn right. Pass Caergwrle Presbyterian church on your left. Go ahead to crossroads at *The Derby Arms*. Cross over the lane and walk down a steep hill to the packhorse bridge over Afon Alun (3).

10. After crossing the bridge, walk uphill and cross a bridge over a railway line. In a few metres, turn left on an enclosed path that runs beside the line. Emerge in a playing field and walk along the left side of it.

11. A few metres before the end of the field, bear left down steps and follow a clear path between the railway and gardens of houses. Emerge onto a road and bear left under a railway bridge. Immediately, turn right on a path to Yr Hob (4) Station.

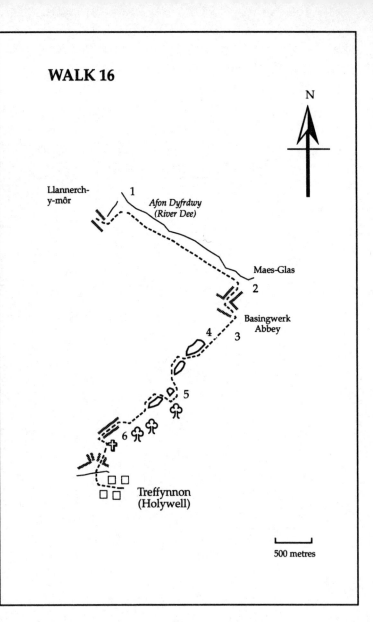

WALK 16

N

Llannerch-y-môr

1

Afon Dyfrdwy
(River Dee)

Maes-Glas

2

Basingwerk
Abbey

4
3

5

6

Treffynnon
(Holywell)

500 metres

Llannerch-y-môr – Basingwerk Abbey
– St Winefride's Well – Treffynnon (Holywell)

Route:	Easy. Level walking beside the Dee estuary followed by tracks and paths through Maes-glas (Greenfield) Heritage Park.
Time:	2½ hours.
Start:	Bus stop at Abakhan Fabrics, Llannerch-y-môr, on the A548, 1½ miles (2.4 km) NW of Maes-glas. GR 176791.
Finish:	Treffynnon (Holywell) Bus Station. GR 187757.
Public Transport:	Bus no. 11 Rhyl-Chester links the start and finish. Nearest railway stations are at Y Fflint and Prestatyn, both are on the no. 11 bus route.
Parking:	Near Treffynnon town centre. Parking at Abakhan Fabrics for customers only (gates locked at 5.30 p.m.)
Facilities:	Cafe at Abakhan. Seasonal cafe near Basingwerk Abbey. Pubs en route and in Treffynnon. Public toilets in the car park at Treffynnon.
OS Maps:	1:50 000 Landranger 116; 1:25 000 Explorer 265.

Points of Interest:

1. The Duke of Lancaster used to operate as a ferry between Heysham and Belfast. Since 1979, the vessel has been moored at Llannerch-y-môr, although the plans to make it into a leisure complex – a *Fun Ship* – have been unsuccessful.

2. In the 18th and 19th centuries, Maes-glas was a busy dock exporting goods from the factories in the valley. There was a passenger sailing ship to Chester and, in 1857, a passenger service was introduced to Prince's Pier at Liverpool. In 1870, *the Holywell and Liverpool Steam Packet Company* built a 130 foot long paddle steamer called St Winefred, which could carry 300 passengers and 40 tons of cargo. Competition from the railway was too great, and the service was short lived. Little remains of the large wharf and, nowadays, the dock is only used by fishing boats.

3. Ranulf, the earl of Chester, founded a Savigniac abbey at Basingwerk in 1131. Sixteen years later, it changed to the Cistercian order. By 1157, there was an abbey on the present site and it soon became a thriving agricultural community. Thomas Pennant, the ancestor of Pennant the Naturalist (see Walk 17), was abbot here in the 15th century. After the dissolution of the abbeys in 1536, it passed to the Mostyn family of Talacre.

4. Built in ten weeks in 1785, the six storey Lower Cotton Mill was powered by an 18 foot waterwheel. The company closed in 1840, and the building remained unused until the 1850s, when it was taken over as a flour mill

5. Known also as the Battery Works, Greenfield Mills was the largest of the industrial sites in the valley. The copper and brass battery mills produced a large number of pans, bowls, kettles and other utensils. Many of the products were exported via Liverpool to the west coast of Africa, where merchants traded the goods in exchange for slaves, who were taken to America and the West Indies. After the works closed in 1894, the site was taken over by several different manufacturers. Some of the buildings were used by a hosiery company until there was a disastrous fire on the site in the 1950s

6. For many centuries, St Winefride's Well has been a place of pilgrimage. According to legend, St Winefride's head was cut

off by Caradoc ap Alyn in the 7th century, when she rejected his advances. St Beuno, her uncle, replaced her head, restoring her to life whilst Caradoc disappeared into the earth. The holy spring rose from the spot where St Winefride's head had fallen. She became abbess of a nunnery at Gwytherin near Llanrwst. Many famous people have visited the shrine, and the 15th century chapel surrounding the well may have been built for Margaret Beaufort, Henry VII's mother.

Walk Directions: (–) denotes Point of Interest

1. With your back to Abakhan Fabrics entrance, go left and ignore the first footpath on the left. In a few paces, bear left at another footpath signpost. Have a stream on your left and go under a low railway bridge.

2. On the other side of the channel is the *Duke of Lancaster* (1). Walk along a track and, at a fence, bear right to a stile. Continue along an embankment to have views of Afon Dyfrdwy (River Dee) on your left.

3. Cross several stiles and a kissing gate on top of the embankment. At its end, climb a stile at a gate and emerge at Maes-glas dock (2).

4. Bear right and join a lane. Keep ahead and cross a bridge over the railway line. On reaching the A548, cross with care. Turn left and bear right on a lane at a footpath signpost. In about 200 metres, you will emerge onto another track, to your left is a cafe, the Heritage Park Visitor Centre and Basingwek Abbey ruins (3).

5. Take the track opposite and pass the grounds of the farm museum on your left. Pass the Environment Centre on your right, then emerge on a lane. Turn left and pass the Abbey Wire Mill site and its mill pond on your right. You will soon see the Lower Cotton Mill (4) on your right.

6. Continue beside the Mill Pool and, when the lane goes uphill, continue on a path beside the lake. Pass a picnic area and go right at a fork. Ignore gates on the right and pass a weir. Go up steps and, half-way up, bear right to cross a bridge and dam. On your right is Meadow Mill.

7. On the opposite side of the dam, go down steps and walk up to a car park. Go through it but, before reaching a road, go left through a kissing gate at a barrier. Walk along a track and pass an old clock tower.

8. Bear left at a fork and, after passing a ruin on the left, turn left. At the next fork, bear right to have the ruins of Greenfield Mills (5) on your right. At a chimney on the left, bear right across a dam.

9. Bear left beside Battery Pool and keep left on the grassy path beside the pool. Emerge near *the Royal Oak* and go left up a stepped, railed path. At the top, turn right on a path and follow it past a chimney to join another path near a kissing gate. Go through it and walk downhill. Pass buildings and emerge on the B5121.

10. Turn left and pass the entrance to St Winefride's Well (6). At St Winefride's chapel, go left through a gate. In a few metres, turn right up a railed path.

11. Walk ahead along a road and pass Plas Dewi flats on your right. Continue uphill to a road junction. Cross directly to Treffynnon shopping precinct and bear left to the bus station.

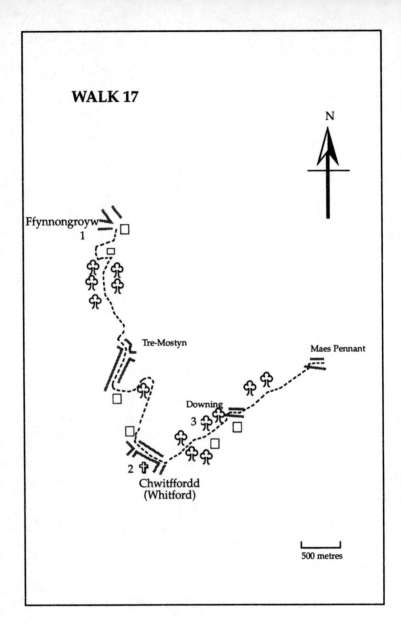

WALK 17

N

Ffynnongroyw
1

Tre-Mostyn

Maes Pennant

Downing

3

2

Chwitffordd
(Whitford)

500 metres

Ffynnongroyw – Chwitffordd (Whitford) – Downing – Maes Pennant

Route:	A gradual climb through attractive woodlands and field to Chwitffordd followed by a walk through the former Downing estate.
Start:	*Llinegar Country Hotel*, Ffynnongroyw, near the A548, opposite a railway footbridge at the eastern end of Ffynnongroyw, where a road from Pen-y-ffordd meets the A548. GR 140820.
Finish:	Maes Pennant. GR 166794.
Public Transport:	Bus no. 11 Rhyl-Chester links Ffynnongroyw with Maes Pennant. Nearest railway stations are Prestatyn and Y Fflint. Both are on the no. 11 bus route.
Parking:	At start, small parking area just before the ford at Garth Mill. At finish, on street parking in Maes Pennant.
Facilities:	Pub at start and in Chwitffordd.
OS Maps:	1:50 000 Landranger 116; 1:25 000 Explorer 265.

Points of Interest:

1. According to local legend, the first inhabitants of Ffynnongroyw were shipwrecked sailors, who discovered the well that gives the village its name. More recently, many of the inhabitants worked at the nearby Point of Ayr colliery or Mostyn Iron Works. Now a public house, Garth Mill dates from the mid 18th century, and it functioned as a water powered cornmill until the 1950s.

2. The church of St Mary and St Beuno in Chwitffordd, was

largely rebuilt in the mid 19th century. Inside is a memorial to Thomas Pennant (1726-98) who lived nearby at Downhill Hall. He is remembered in Wales for his published works *A Tour in Wales* and *History of Whiteford and Holywell*. He was known in Europe for his work on zoology and he corresponded with the Swedish botanist Carl Linnaeus and Gilbert White of Selborne. On the NE side of the churchyard is the grave of the self-taught artist Moses Griffith, who accompanied Thomas Pennant on his travels. About a mile west of the village, stands Maen Achwyfan. Ornamented with intricate patterns, the tall Celtic cross is about 1000 years old.

3. Almost nothing remains of Downing Hall. Built in 1627, it was the home of the Pennant family until the 19th century. One of their ancestors was Thomas Pennant, the last abbot of Basingwerk Abbey. The estate, consisting of the hall, 12,000 acres and stabling for 12 horses, was sold off in 1920, but two years later the house was destroyed by fire. It was demolished in 1953. The stable block, built in 1766, still stands.

Walk Directions: (–) denotes Point of Interest

1. At the east end of Ffynnongroyw (1), have *the Llinegar Country Hotel* on your left and turn left up Garth Lane. Pass a small parking area and cross a footbridge. Pass Garth Mill on your left and, immediately, go left to pass behind the mill.

2. Follow a path as it rises gradually through a wooded valley. Pass above the former mill pond and, after the confluence of the rivers, the Nant Felin Blwm. Ignore paths leading off on the left. Higher up, you will pass rhododendrons and a ruin on your right. Go through a gate across the path and emerge onto a track.

3. Turn right and cross a stile at a gate. Go ahead, slightly left to another stile. Cross the narrow field to another stile and continue beside a right-hand fence and trees. Cross a stile at a

gate and emerge onto a lane at Tre-Mostyn. Turn left and, after 100 metres, bear right on another lane.

4. Walk uphill and, after 600 metres, turn left through gates at farm buildings. Pass between barns and go through the gate ahead on to a hedged track. Follow it to the edge of a wood then turn left through a gate.

5. With the wood on your right, continue along a track. A few posts with yellow arrows mark the route. In about 500 metres, the track curves to the right and arrives at a small open space. Ignore a bridleway on the left and continue right to go through a gate into a field.

6. Bear right through the large field, but gradually veer left away from the wood. Join a track near a bend and bear right along it to a gate and cattlegrid near a lodge.

7. Turn left on the lane and ignore another lane on the right. Walk into the village of Chwitffordd (2) and pass the church on your right. At a road on your right, go left along Upper Downing Road.

8. Continue along Altbridge Care Home drive. Pass a field on your right and enter trees. Ignore a footpath on your right and, just before a left bend in the drive, cross a stile on your right.

9. Follow a wet path through the trees and cross above a stream. Walk up a track and bear right to pass the former Downing stables on your right. At the drive, where there is a gate on your right, turn left and pass a clearing, the site of Downing Hall (3), on your left.

10. Follow the track to a stile. Continue ahead and, at gates, go left on a short path to a stile. Turn right on the lane and, in a few paces, go left on a track.

11. Follow the bridleway as it curves to the right through a field

to a gate. Continue past trees to a small gate and the road at Maes Pennant. Turn right to the bus stops.

WALK 18

N

Gronant Dunes

3

Point of Ayr

□ 2

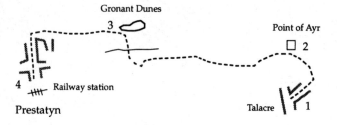

4

⊣⊦⊦ Railway station

Prestatyn

Talacre

1

500 metres

Talacre – Gronant Dunes
– Barkby Beach – Prestatyn

Route:	Easy-moderate. Dune paths and beach.
Start:	Bus stop at *Talacre Beach Country Club*. GR 121844.
Finish:	Prestatyn Railway Station. GR 063830, or Bus Station. GR 064829.
Public Transport:	Bus no. 101 Rhyl-Prestatyn – *Talacre Beach Club* operates from mid May to early September. Bus no. 11 Rhyl-Prestatyn-Chester to Talacre Station Road End, about 1 mile from start. From Prestatyn, buses to Rhyl and Chester. Prestatyn is on the north Wales coast railway line.
Parking:	Car park near the end of the road in Talacre. Several car parks in Prestatyn.
Facilities:	Refreshments in Talacre and Prestatyn. Public toilets near the start and at Barkby Beach.
OS Maps:	1:50 000 Landranger 116; 1:25 000 Explorer 265.

Points of Interest:

1. The Dee estuary is an internationally important nature reserve for birds over-wintering or resting whilst on migration. In the winter, more than 100,000 waders and ducks feed on the mudflats and saltmarshes. Talacre and Gronant dunes are all that remain of a dune system that once stretched from the Point of Ayr to Afon Clwyd. Established in 1865, the Point of Ayr colliery did not close until 1996. Pit ponies brought the coal to the surface. There is now a gas terminal in the area.

2. The present lighthouse at Talacre was built in 1819, to replace one that was established in 1777. Having a height of 99 feet, the lighthouse's blinking light was visible 19 miles away. Since it closed, the building has been a wartime lookout and a holiday home. Talacre used to have a lifeboat station and, by the time it closed in 1923, the crews had saved 476 lives.

3. Gronant Dunes is a designated local nature reserve. The dunes support a variety of insects and plants whilst waders and cormorants may be seen on the foreshore. The reserve has the only breeding colony of little terns in Wales. Moorhen, coot, various warblers and reed bunting, may be spotted on or around the Gutter.

4. The history of Prestatyn dates from prehistoric times. A skeleton, thought to be Neolithic, was discovered below the High Street in 1924. On the south side of the town is a small Roman bathhouse. There was a castle on the coastal plain on the east side of the town. It was taken by Owain Gwynedd in the mid 12th century. After the coming of the railway, Prestatyn grew into a coastal resort. Offa's Dyke long distance path ends (or starts if you are walking north to south) near the seashore.

Walk Directions: (–) denotes Point of Interest

1. At the bus stop, face *Talacre Beach Country Club* and turn right along the pavement. Ignore all roads turning off. Pass the *Smuggler's Inn* and a car park and ignore a footpath on the left.

2. On reaching an embankment overlooking the Dee estuary (1), turn left through a kissing gate. In about 150 metres, bear left on another path. Follow posts through the dunes in the direction of the beach. After veering left, pass through a gap in a fence to reach the beach and Point of Ayr lighthouse (2).

3. Return to the footpath signpost at the back of the beach and bear right. Walk between fences to a large open space backed

by high dunes. Bear right beside a fence and, when it ends at a corner, follow the bridleway signs.

4. The track bears to the left and joins a concrete track. Ignore a left-hand track at a fenced Dunes Conservation Area. On reaching another bridleway sign, which points to the left, turn right on a concrete track. It soon becomes grassy. Continue along it as it bears left and, in a dip, go right over a sandhill to the beach.

5. Turn left along the beach and ignore paths going left to Presthaven Sands. In about a kilometre, you will have reeds on your right near the mouth of Prestatyn Gutter.

6. Walk along the shingle and continue along a path. Ignore a path on the left and pass a sandhill with trees on the left. Continue with the stream nearby on your right.

7. Eventually, the path veers away from Prestatyn Gutter to pass behind caravans. It returns to the stream but, in a few more metres, goes left between fences to a gate near Presthaven Sands. Immediately, bear right through a kissing gate into Twyni Gronant Dunes Nature Reserve (3).

8. Follow the path ahead but soon bear right on a lesser path to a footbridge over Prestatyn Gutter. Walk ahead until the path reaches a (possibly dried-up) pool. Turn left on a path beside it, and maintain your direction through the dunes.

9. In about a kilometre, the path passes above Barkby Beach. Follow a right-hand fence to a viewing platform, then descend to the beach. Walk beside a fence to the promenade and car park.

10. Continue along the promenade to another car park at Prestatyn Central Beach (4). Walk out to Bastion Road and follow it to a crossroads. Cross directly, and you will shortly arrive at the railway station. For the bus station, cross the footbridge and, after passing a few shops, turn right.

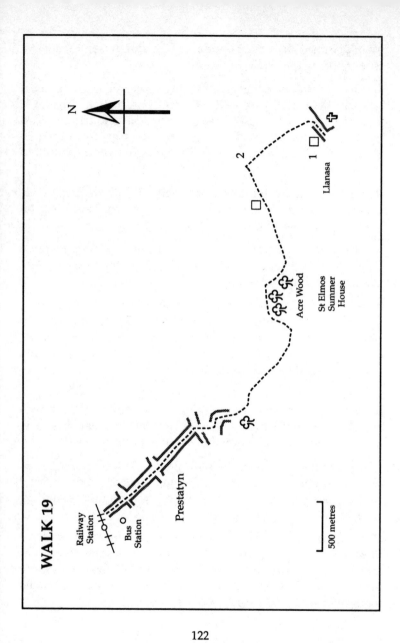

WALK 19

N

Railway Station
Bus Station

Prestatyn

Acre Wood

St Elmos
Summer
House

Llanasa

1

2

500 metres

Llanasa – Acre Wood – Prestatyn

Route:	Easy-moderate. Tracks and hillside paths. A gradual climb at the start but much of the walk is downhill.
Time:	2 hours.
Start:	Llanasa. Bus stop near the church and *Red Lion*. GR 106814.
Finish:	Prestatyn Railway Station. GR 063830.
Public Transport:	To the start, take Rural Rider Bus no. H2 Holywell-Prestatyn. Stops in Llanasa by request. Ask the driver or phone (P & O Lloyd) 01352 710682.
Parking:	Car parks off Prestatyn High Street.
Facilities:	Pub in Llanasa. Full facilities in Prestatyn.
OS Maps:	1:50 000 Landranger 116; 1:25 000 Explorer 265.

Points of Interest:

1. Llanasa has its origin in the 6th century when the second bishop of Llanelwy (St Asaph) built a church here.

The present church dates from the 16th century and has a magnificent east window. A plaque in the church commemorates the bravery of the Point of Ayr lifeboat crew of thirteen, who lost their lives in a gale in 1857 during an attempt to save the men on board the Irish schooner *Temperance* off the coast, near Abergele. John Jones, who became known as *Poet Jones* in England, was born in Llanasa in 1788. The son of a poor farmer, he was sent, at the age of eight, to work in the cotton mills of Dougles and Smalley in Treffynnon. He joined the navy in 1804 and, at the end of the Napoleonic Wars, returned to the mills. He went to work in a cotton mill in Stalybridge when he was thirty-two, and stayed there until he died in 1858. During this time, when he suffered from ill health, he wrote many poems. Writing in English, he tells of the cruelty of the Holywell mills: *'Rods, doomed to bruise in barbarous dens of noise The tender form of orphan girls and boys.'*

2. The lighthouse at the Point of Ayr was replaced in the 19th century by a lightship which guided ships into Liverpool Bay and the ports in the Dee estuary. The estuary is now an important nature reserve and many species of wader spend the winter here.

Walk Directions: (–) denotes Point of Interest

1. From the bus stop near the church in Llanasa (1), walk towards the *Red Lion*. At the road junction, bear right and, in about 150 metres, turn left along a dead-end lane. Ignore a track and footpath on the right. Near the lane end are good views of the Dee estuary and Point of Ayr lighthouse (2).

2. Turn left on a bridleway. When the track bears right to a house, maintain your direction. Further on, the bridleway narrows into a path and passes a ruin. Ignore footpaths leading off and follow the bridleway to where it emerges on a track near a ruined house.

3. Turn left on the track and pass coniferous trees on the left. On reaching a mast on the right, bear left along the track and, in another 200 metres, you will see stiles on the left and right. To your left once stood St Elmo's Summerhouse on the old Golden Grove Estate.

4. Cross the stile on the right and slant to the left across the field to a stile. Continue slightly left and descend through the field to the next stile. Cross and walk on to a stile on the right and great views of the coast. Head downhill until a fence is in front of you and then bear left beside it to a stile in the corner.

Cross and bear right along the field boundary to a stile. Walk ahead through trees until you emerge on a road at a bend.

5. Turn right and walk downhill. Follow the road around a bend and, in about another 50 metres, bear right on a surfaced path. Cross a drive and continue downhill until you reach a road.

6. Turn left and, almost immediately, bear right and follow a road downhill to a road junction at *The Cross Foxes* in Prestatyn. Cross the road and maintain your direction along the High Street to the railway station.

WALK 20

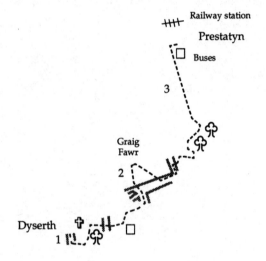

Railway station

Prestatyn

Buses

3

Graig
Fawr

2

Dyserth

1

500 metres

Dyserth – Graig Fawr – Prestatyn

Route:	Easy-moderate. Gradual climb to Graig Fawr followed by a short section of Offa's Dyke Path then level walking.
Time:	2-2½ hours.
Start:	Dyserth. Bus stop near the *Red Lion* and Dyserth waterfall. GR 056793.
Finish:	Prestatyn Bus Station or Railway Station. GR 064830.
Public Transport:	To the start, take bus no. 36 from Rhyl or no. 35 from Prestatyn. From the finish, buses to Rhyl and Chester. Prestatyn is on the north Wales coast railway line.
Parking:	Car parks off Prestatyn High Street. Car parks near the waterfall and bus stops in Dyserth.
Facilities:	Pub and seasonal cafe in Dyserth. Public toilets in the car park. Full facilities in Prestatyn.
OS Maps:	1:50 000 Landranger 116; 1:25 000 Explorer 265.

Points of Interest:

1. Dyserth was mentioned in the *Domesday Book* of 1086 and, at that time, it had a church and a mill. Dedicated to St Cwyfan and St Bridget, the present church was rebuilt in Victorian times by Gilbert Scott, but it has a medieval stained glass window. Dyserth is also known for its spectacular 60 foot waterfall which flows from Ffynnon Asa (St Asaph's well). Henry III built a castle near Dyserth in 1241, but Llywelyn ap Gruffudd destroyed it in 1263.

2. Graig Fawr was given to the National Trust by Sir Geoffrey Summers of *Shotton Steelworks*. The remains of old mineral workings lie below the hill. The Talargoch lead and zinc mine was one of the most important in the area, but the high cost of keeping the mine dry forced its closure in 1884. Graig Fawr is rich in lime-loving plants, such as wild thyme and common rockrose. The summit provides a fine viewpoint and, on a clear day, views stretch west beyond the Vale of Clwyd to the distant peaks of Eryri (Snowdonia). Nearer, to the south, is Y Foel and the forested Mynydd y Cwm. Wooded Gop Hill with its prehistoric cairn is to the east, whilst in the north is the sprawl of Prestatyn and Meliden.

3. The trackbed of the Dyserth Railway is now a recreational footpath called the Prestatyn Walkway. *The London and North Western Railway Company* owned the line and opened it in 1867 to transport minerals from the local mines and quarries. A passenger service operated from 1905 until 1930. The last mineral trains stopped running in 1973, although the limestone quarry at Dyserth did not close until 1981.

Walk Directions: (–) denotes Point of Interest

1. From the bus stop near the *Red Lion* in Dyserth (1), pass the entrance to the waterfall on your left and, in a few paces, bear left. Climb a stepped path and ignore a right-hand fork. Pass houses and walk up to a lane end. Immediately, go left on a path and descend to a footbridge.

2. Continue on a board walk to a path and follow it through trees. Climb a stile across the path and turn right on a path that goes up to a field. Walk ahead to a waymarked post beside trees. Continue ahead, slightly right, towards trees that jut into the field. Cross a stile at the corner of the woodland and take a path between fences to a lane.

3. Cross the lane and climb steps to a stile and kissing gate.

Follow the path ahead to a track and cross a bridge over the old railway line. Climb a stile and walk along a path towards the left side of a house. Cross a path and go on ahead, through trees. Cross a stile and emerge onto a track.

4. Turn left and, at a fork, bear left. On reaching a gate, don't go through, but bear right to have a fence on your left. Climb a stile at a gate and cross a field to another. Emerge on a lane and turn left.

5. Ignore a lane on the left and, in a few metres, at a junction, turn left, then bear right into a parking area. Take the path ahead for about 200 metres then bear left to the summit of Graig Fawr (2). On the return, do not go back to the car park, instead take a path towards a gate that is opposite a house with three brick chimneys.

6. Turn left onto the lane and, in about 200 metres, turn left onto another lane. In a few metres, bear right on the Offa's Dyke Path. Pass through a kissing gate and follow a track. Before reaching gates to a house, go through a kissing gate on the right. The path bends right to have a quarry below on the left.

7. Leave the Offa's Dyke Path at a path junction and bear left downhill through trees to a kissing gate. Join an access lane and follow it for about 200 metres. Ignore the stile in front of you and turn right on a track that soon becomes a path.

8. The path enters Coed yr Esgob. Keep to the lower path at a junction of paths and have a fence on the left. It passes below a house. Go down steps onto the golf course – take care – and cross to the old railway track (3).

9. Turn right along it and pass below the A547 and another road. Continue ahead at a junction. Emerge onto a road and cross it to another stretch of surfaced track. Pass a barrier and turn right. In about 100 metres, bear right to Prestatyn bus

station. For the railway station, cross the road to the next street then turn left.